MW00889882

Discover Secret Gems in Illinois: Insider Guide

Raya .W Bush

All rights reserved.

Copyright © 2024 Raya .W Bush

Discover Secret Gems in Illinois: Insider Guide : Uncover Hidden Wonders of Illinois with this Must-Have Guide

.

Funny helpful tips:

Stay vigilant about tech's impact on mental health; while it connects us, it also poses challenges like screen addiction.

Stay authentic; your unique essence is your strength.

Introduction

Embark on an unforgettable journey through the diverse landscapes and cultural gems of Illinois with this book. Discover the hidden treasures and offbeat destinations that make the Land of Lincoln a must-visit destination.

Begin your exploration with a visit to the stunning Chain O'Lakes State Park, offering picturesque views and outdoor adventures. Immerse yourself in the natural beauty of Bell Smith Springs, Shawnee National Forest, and Cache River Natural Area. Experience the wonders of Giant City State Park, Inspiration Point, and the breathtaking Little Grand Canyon.

For urban explorers, Chicago beckons with iconic landmarks such as the 360 Chicago Observation Deck, Art Institute of Chicago, and the historic Chicago Theatre. Enjoy the serenity of the Lakefront Trail, explore the Lincoln Park Zoo, and relax at the beautiful Maggie Daley Park. Take in the city's skyline from the 360 Chicago Observation Deck or the Willis Tower Skydeck.

Dive into Chicago's rich cultural scene with visits to the Field Museum, Shedd Aquarium, and the Museum of Science and Industry. Stroll along Navy Pier, North Avenue Beach, and the Lakefront Trail for a perfect blend of nature and city life.

Venture beyond Chicago to discover the beauty of White Pines Forest State Park, Dixon Springs State Park, and the enchanting Cave-In-Rock. Marvel at the natural wonders of Garden of the Gods, Lighthouse Beach, and Cahokia Mounds State Historic Site.

Whether you're a nature enthusiast, history buff, or urban explorer, this book has something for everyone. From waterfalls and state parks to historic sites and cultural attractions, this guide ensures that your Illinois adventure is filled with unforgettable experiences. Pack your bags, hit the road, and let the Land of Lincoln captivate you with its charm and diversity.

Contents

About Illinois

Illinois is a state with one of the country's most diverse landscapes. Illinois is home to many natural resources in its southern portion, various farmlands and agriculture sites in the northern and central areas, and the vast and influential city of Chicago in the northeast. The Mississippi River makes up its western border, while the Ohio River is on the southern border.

Illinois takes its name from what French Catholic missionaries used when referencing the natives in the seventeenth century. "Illinois" is believed to be from the Miami-Illinois verb for "who speaks the regular way."

Illinois land was once held by various American Indian tribes, although most of them left in the fifteenth century due to a lack of resources. French explorers established settlements in the area in the seventeenth and eighteenth centuries to escape British rule. The Illinois territory was transferred to the British in 1763 following the Seven Years' War. It would be ceded to the United States in the 1780s, becoming part of the Northwest Territory.

Illinois became the country's twenty-first state in 1818. The city of Springfield was named Illinois's capital in 1837. Chicago also grew in the nineteenth century as a critical port to the Great Lakes and remains the state's largest city.

Today, Illinois is home to about 12.8 million people, making it the sixth most populated state in the U.S. The state has been influential in many ways. John Deere built his first steel plow in Illinois in the 1830s. The Manhattan Project operated out of the University of Chicago in the 1940s, developing the first controlled nuclear chain reaction. The first McDonald's restaurant also opened in Illinois in the 1960s.

Illinois has a strong presidential history as well. Abraham Lincoln, Ulysses Grant, and Barack Obama all lived in Illinois when they were elected to the presidency. Ronald Reagan was also born in the state and grew up there before moving to California.

Landscape and Climate

Illinois is divided into three sections. Northern Illinois features the Chicago area and the cities of Rockford, Rock Island, and Moline.

Central Illinois is a prairie region of the state and is home to many agricultural and manufacturing sites. The soybean and corn industries are among the most prominent in Central Illinois. Peoria, Springfield, Champaign, Decatur, and Quincy are the top cities here.

Southern Illinois is the least-populated part of the state. The region is home to a vast coal mining industry, but there are many agriculture farms throughout the area as well. You'll find the Shawnee National Forest and a connection between the Ohio and Mississippi Rivers here. Some of the cities in Southern Illinois include Marion, Carbondale, and the eastern St. Louis suburbs of Edwardsville, Belleville, O'Fallon, and Alton.

The climate in Illinois is humid, with the southern half of the state being warmer on average. Tornadoes can occur in the southern end of the state, although they aren't as powerful or frequent as what people may find in Missouri or Iowa.

Temperatures can reach the 80s and 90s in the summer, and the lowest temperatures can fall to nearly 10°F in the winter. The state experiences about 51 days of storm activity each year on average. The Chicago area can get around 40 inches of snow in a year, while other parts of the state will see about 15 inches.

Chain O'Lakes State Park

The Chain O'Lakes State Park is in the middle of one of the state's largest groupings of lakes. The park borders the Nippersink, Grass, and Marie lakes, while the Turner Lake is at the western end. It offers four trail systems and three loops for horseback riding to the west. There is also a boat-launching area to the south near Catfish Cove.

The park has an archery range in the north. Ice fishing is also available around some of the lakes during the winter season.

Best Time to Visit: Visit during the fall, as the weather conditions will be pleasant enough for most activities here.

Pass/Permit/Fees: It costs $25 to reserve a camping site for the night. You can also rent a boat or horse for riding, but the costs for these rentals will vary by season.

Closest City or Town: Antioch

How to Get There: From Antioch, head west on Lake St toward Victoria and turn right onto IL-173 W. Turn left onto Johnsburg Wilmot Rd and then take another left in 1.6 miles. Continue onto Chain-O-Lakes State Park.

GPS Coordinates: 42.45795° N, 88.18932° W

Did You Know? The waters around the park feature largemouth bass, muskie, catfish, white bass, and many other fish. However, most fishing occurs on piers, as the water contains too much marsh for many boats.

Bell Smith Springs

You'll find the Bell Smith Springs tucked in the eastern part of Pope County in the Shawnee National Forest. The springs feature many beautiful streams and canyons surrounded by tall sandstone cliffs.

There are 8 miles of walking trails throughout Bell Smith Springs. The trails are populated by many forms of wildlife, including deer, wild turkeys, and bobcats.

Best Time to Visit: The summer is the best time to visit, as the waters are warm enough to where you can go swimming in some of the shallow parts of the springs.

Pass/Permit/Fees: It costs $10 to rent a campsite for the night. You can bring up to two vehicles and eight people here.

Closest City or Town: Bloomfield

How to Get There: From Bloomfield, head north on Renfro Rd and turn right onto US-45 N. In 8.8 miles, take a right onto Ozark Road and turn right to stay on Ozark Road for eight more miles. Turn right and then continue onto Bell Smith Springs Rd to reach the scenic area.

GPS Coordinates: 37.51955° N, 88.65830° W

Did You Know? Look for the stone arch at the springs near the Natural Bridge Trail. The arch is the largest in the Shawnee National Forest at about 125 feet long.

Shawnee National Forest

The Shawnee National Forest in southern Illinois is on nearly a quarter of a million acres of land. The forest features rock formations created by the Laurentide Ice Sheet that covered much of Illinois more than 100,000 years ago. The forest houses various sites of interest, such as the Little Grand Canyon and Cedar Lake in the northwestern area. Devil's Kitchen Lake is in the central area.

The area offers various hiking spaces, including a 160-mile trail that is part of the American Discovery Trail. You'll also find a few mountain-biking trails around the park, and the Jackson Falls campsite also features a few rock-climbing spaces.

Best Time to Visit: Avoid visiting between October and January, if possible, as it is hunting season during that time.

Pass/Permit/Fees: It is free to visit the forest, but you will need to pay to reserve a campsite.

Closest City or Town: Bloomfield

How to Get There: From Bloomfield, head north on Renfro Rd and turn left onto Shelby Rd. Turn left onto US-45 S. In 1.4 miles, turn right onto Holley Rd, right onto Dutchman Lake Rd, and left onto Fishing Hole Ln to reach Dutchman Lake Falls trail in Shawnee National Forest.

GPS Coordinates: 37.49618° N, 88.91097° W

Did You Know? The forest was featured on a quarter coin that was issued in 2016.

The Morton Arboretum

You'll find thousands of trees at the Morton Arboretum in Lisle. The compound has 1,700 acres of land with more than 4,000 plant species. The arboretum has exhibits highlighting how trees grow and propagate. There is also an exhibit on threatened and endangered trees here. The grounds feature various trees and plants in multiple gardens. The park also contains a children's garden where children can interact with some of the plants on display. The arboretum also offers a tram service to bring people to and from different parts of the park, often passing Joe the Guardian, a massive statue looking over the southern end of the park.

Best Time to Visit: The arboretum offers discounted admission on Wednesdays.

Pass/Permit/Fees: Admission is $16 for adults, $14 for seniors, and $11 for children. All ticket prices drop by a few dollars on Wednesdays.

Closest City or Town: Bolingbrook

How to Get There: In Bolingbrook, take I-55 N toward Chicago and then exit 269 to merge onto I-355 N. Keep right at the fork to stay on I-355 N and use the right lanes to take exit 20 A to merge onto I-88 W. Take exit 130 for IL-53 N and then turn right onto Ginkgo Way to reach 4100 IL-53.

GPS Coordinates: 41.81654° N, 88.06331° W

Did You Know? Dogs can enter, but it costs $5 for each dog, and they must be on a leash at all times.

Cache River Natural Area

You'll find the Cache River Natural Area in the Johnson County town of Belknap in southern Illinois. The area is in a floodplain formed by glacial floodwater from the nearby Ohio River centuries ago.

You'll find some of the most massive cypress trees in the Cache River Natural Area. The trees feature bases that are more than 40 feet in circumference. Some of them are over a thousand years old.

The natural area offers a bike trail that leads to the Tunnel Hill State Trail, a 48-mile trail that links to Harrisburg.

Best Time to Visit: The spring and fall are the best times to visit, as the weather conditions will be more favorable.

Pass/Permit/Fees: It is free to visit the natural area.

Closest City or Town: Cairo

How to Get There: From Cairo, take IL-37 N for 13.7 miles and turn right onto IL-169 E. In 2.7 miles, turn left onto E 1st St. Continue onto Franklin St and then Karnak Rd. Take a left onto E Main St and a right onto Clark St/Sunflower Ln to reach 930 Sunflower Ln.

GPS Coordinates: 37.33107° N, 88.94029° W

Did You Know? The area features multiple soils and ecological regions that support a wide variety of living things.

Giant City State Park

You will find the Giant City State Park south of Carbondale in the town of Makanda. The park is in the middle of the River to River Trail in Illinois between the Ohio and Mississippi rivers.

The park features more than 70 types of trees. You can learn about these various trees and other growths here at the visitor center. There's a 12-mile horseback-riding loop at the park, and nearby stables offer horses that people can rent for a ride along the trail. You can also reserve one of the many camping spaces in the area, one of which is dedicated to youth camping.

Best Time to Visit: The fall is a good time to visit when the conditions are not as humid.

Pass/Permit/Fees: The cost for renting a campsite or a horse for riding will vary throughout the year.

Closest City or Town: Carbondale

How to Get There: In Carbaondale, hea south on US-51 S and then turn left onto Makanda Rd. Take a slight right onto Baptist Hill Rd, continue onto S Church Rd, and then turn left onto Giant City Rd to reach the park on the right at 235 Giant City Rd.

GPS Coordinates: 37.60628° N, 89.18593° W

Did You Know? One of the camping spots here is a primitive campground with very few amenities. You can pitch a tent on any space, provided it is far from a designated road.

Inspiration Point

Inspiration Point is on the southwestern end of Illinois near the Big Muddy River and Tower Island Chute, near the Mississippi River. The point is part of the Shawnee National Forest.

Inspiration Point is a rock formation featuring various limestone formations. The area surrounds a vast forest space with a short trail offering many views.

Best Time to Visit: Visit during sunset for some of the most dynamic natural views you'll find in the state.

Pass/Permit/Fees: It is free to enter the forest.

Closest City or Town: Carbondale

How to Get There: From Carbondale, take Old Highway 13 west from the city and then head south onto IL-127 S. Turn right onto Pomona Rd, right onto Natural Bridge Rd, and then take a slight left onto Jerusalem Hill Rd. In 2.8 miles, take a right onto Macedonia Rd and then a left to stay on Macedonia Rd. Take a slight left onto Hutchins Creek Rd, a slight right onto Scatters Rd, and then continue onto Larue Rd. Turn left onto Pine Hills Rd, and the trailhead for Inspiration Point is on the left.

GPS Coordinates: 37.58583° N, 89.43600° W

Did You Know? You'll find a small picnic area near the northern end of the surrounding hiking trail.

Little Grand Canyon

The northwestern end of the Shawnee National Forest is home to the Little Grand Canyon, a small box canyon featuring about 3 miles of hiking trails.

Visitors will see the natural erosion from the nearby Big Muddy River. The bluffs around the canyon are about 300 feet tall, with a small creek surrounded by vast forest space. The trail features a steep surface that provides a challenge to hikers of all skill levels.

Best Time to Visit: April and October are the best months to visit. You'll see plenty of wildflowers in bloom in April, while the fall colors will be their most noticeable in October.

Pass/Permit/Fees: It is free to visit the canyon, but no overnight camping is allowed. You cannot bring any off-road vehicles or horses to the trail.

Closest City or Town: Carbondale

How to Get There: From Carbondale, head west on Old Highway 13 and then take a left on IL-127. Take a right on Hoffman Road, then go left on Hickory Ridge Road, continuing south until you reach the canyon parking area in Pomona, IL.

GPS Coordinates: 37.68441° N, 89.40163° W

Did You Know? You'll find bobcats, foxes, deer, raccoons, and many other forms of wildlife while at the canyon.

Little Grassy Lake

Little Grassy Lake is a small reservoir in Jackson and Williamson counties in southern Illinois near Carbondale. The reservoir comes from a dam near the Little Grassy Creek. The area features about 1,200 acres of land and nearly 36 miles of shore. The lake is ideal for warm-water fishing, including largemouth bass. Kayaking, paddle boarding, and canoeing are also available throughout the year.

Best Time to Visit: The spring is an ideal time to visit, as the temperatures won't be as intense at this point in the year.

Pass/Permit/Fees: It costs $20 to rent a single-person kayak for 3 hours or $40 to rent one for the entire day. You can also rent a paddle board, canoe, or pontoon boat for the day. You must provide a $250 security deposit for a pontoon boat, plus you need to make a reservation before arriving.

Closest City or Town: Carbondale

How to Get There: From Carbondale, head east on W Walnut Street and take a slight right onto E Walnut St. Turn right onto S Giant City Rd and left onto Touch of Nature Rd to reach Little Grassy Lake.

GPS Coordinates: 37.64384° N, 89.15173° W

Did You Know? Much of the land where the lake is now was once covered in hickory and oak trees. The area did not provide enough potential for farming, resulting in efforts to dam the creek and produce the lake.

360 Chicago Observation Deck

The 94th floor of the John Hancock Center on North Michigan Avenue in Chicago is home to one of the city's most exciting observation decks. The 360 Chicago Observation Deck provides views of the city in all directions from about 1,000 feet above street level. You'll see the Loop from the south, the Gold Coast from the north, and Navy Pier from the east.

The deck is also home to the Tilt, a thrill ride that extends viewers over the Magnificent Mile, hanging over the city at a 30-degree angle. The deck also features a bar called Bar 94.

Best Time to Visit: Visit about half an hour before sunset for dynamic views.

Pass/Permit/Fees: It costs $30 for a ticket to the deck. You can add a drink at Bar 94 or a ride on the Tilt for $5 extra when you order your ticket.

Closest City or Town: Chicago

How to Get There: In Chicago, head north on S Federal St and turn right onto W Jackson Blvd. Take a left onto S Dearborn St, a right onto W Wacker Dr, a left onto N Michigan Ave, and a right onto E Delaware Pl to reach the observation deck at 875 N Michigan Ave 94th floor.

GPS Coordinates: 41.89902° N, 87.62348° W

Did You Know? The John Hancock Center was the world's second-tallest building when it was constructed in 1968. At 1,127 feet, it is still the city's fifth-tallest tower.

Art Institute of Chicago

The Art Institute of Chicago is a famed art museum noted for housing many of the world's most iconic paintings. The museum features more than 300,000 works in its collection, with exhibits devoted to European, American, African, and Asian art. There's also a modern art section and another devoted to prints. Georges Seurat's *A Sunday Afternoon on the Island of La Grande Jatte* is the most famous painting here. Grant Wood's *American Gothic* and Edward Hopper's *Nighthawks* are among the other famous paintings on display. The museum also houses works from Cassatt, Picasso, Van Gogh, Monet, Warhol, and Pollock. The museum has two lion statues guarding the entrance.

Best Time to Visit: The museum hosts various exhibitions, so check first to see what's appearing here before you visit.

Pass/Permit/Fees: Admission is $25 for adults and $19 for children. Extra tickets for some exhibitions may be required.

Closest City or Town: Chicago

How to Get There: In Chicago, head north on S Federal St and then turn right onto W Jackson Blvd. Take a left onto S Michigan Ave to reach the art institute on the right at 111 S Michigan Ave.

GPS Coordinates: 41.87978° N, 87.62372° W

Did You Know? The Art Institute of Chicago's building was erected for the 1893 World's Columbian Exposition. It is one of the few buildings still left from the fair.

Buckingham Fountain

Buckingham Fountain is one of Chicago's most iconic landmarks. The fountain is in the middle of Grant Park on the shoreline. The Beaux-Arts fountain was built in 1927 and holds about 1.5 million gallons of water.

Buckingham Fountain features a Georgia pink marble body with a distinct green color. The bottom pool is nearly 300 feet in diameter, with plenty of small jets surrounding the center of the fountain.

Best Time to Visit: The fountain operates from April to October and is decorated with lights during the Christmas season when the water is not running. When it's running, the fountain produces a water show at the top of the hour each day, shooting thousands of gallons of water through nearly 200 jets.

Pass/Permit/Fees: You can visit the fountain for free.

Closest City or Town: Chicago

How to Get There: In Chicago, head north on S Federal St and then turn right onto W Jackson Blvd. Take another right onto S Columbus Dr and the fountain is at 301 S Columbus Dr. To reach the closest parking lot continue down S Columbus Dr and the Grant Bark Park lot is on the right.

GPS Coordinates: 41.87599° N, 87.61895° W

Did You Know? The fountain is a few blocks from the western end of Historic Route 66, which is on Michigan Avenue and Jackson Drive.

Chicago River

The Chicago River flows through the middle of downtown Chicago and is one of the most iconic sites to visit while in the city. You can see some of Chicago's most famous buildings from a cruise or kayak ride on the river, including the Merchandise Mart, the Wrigley Building, and the Marina City Towers. Many of the bridges that cross the Chicago River will also lift upward on occasion to make room for some of the boats. These include bridges on Wells, Clark, Dearborn, and State streets.

Best Time to Visit: Visit on St. Patrick's Day, as the city adds green dye to the river that day to create a unique emerald-green look.

Pass/Permit/Fees: The cost of a boat cruise on the river or to rent a kayak for paddling will vary by vendor. You can find many of these vendors throughout the river area.

Closest City or Town: Chicago

How to Get There: In Chicago, head north on S Federal St, turn right onto W Jackson Blvd, and then turn left onto S Columbus Dr. Take a slight left to reach the Millennium Park Garage at 5 S Columbus Dr. To reach the Chicago Riverwalk from the parking garage, you can either access the walk from E Monroe St or Maggie Daley Park.

GPS Coordinates: 41.88558° N, 87.61974° W

Did You Know? The Chicago River flows west from Lake Michigan. The city uses a few canals and control structures to reverse the natural eastern flow of the river, ensuring the city has enough water for use.

Chicago Theatre

The Chicago Theatre on North State Street is one of Chicago's most iconic art institutions. You'll notice the theater with its massive red marquee. The performing arts theater building opened in 1921 and has a capacity of 3,600 people. The structure's auditorium features many detailed chandeliers, while a five-story grand lobby welcomes visitors. The elaborate design of the theater makes for a memorable place to visit. The theater also houses a massive Wurlitzer organ. The organ was installed here in 1921 and remains one of the oldest in operation.

Best Time to Visit: Visit during off-peak hours when there are no events at the theater. Check with the venue to see what is playing before you visit.

Pass/Permit/Fees: Tours are available and cost $18 per person.

Closest City or Town: Chicago

How to Get There: In Chicago, head east on W Jackson Blvd and turn left onto S Michigan Ave. Take a slight left to reach the closest parking garage, Grant Park North Garage. From the garage, head south and take a left onto S Michigan Ave, turn left onto E Washington St and then right onto N State St. It's a ten-minute walk to the theatre.

GPS Coordinates: 41.88579° N, 87.62755° W

Did You Know? In addition to being a performing arts theater, the Chicago Theatre operated as a movie palace until the 1980s. It still hosts some events for the Chicago International Film Festival.

Field Museum

You will find the Field Museum on Chicago's Museum Campus in the South Loop area off of Lake Michigan. The natural history museum highlights many unique wonders of the natural world. Its halls feature models of various animals, including the Tsavo Man-Eater lions. There are also exhibits about ancient Egypt and the evolution of the planet. The most prominent feature at the Field Museum is Sue, a Tyrannosaurus rex skeleton. At about 40 feet long and 13 feet high, it is one of the world's largest dinosaur skeletons. It is also one of the world's most complete skeletons, as 90 percent of its body is intact.

Best Time to Visit: The Field Museum hosts many touring exhibits, so check with the museum to see what is there.

Pass/Permit/Fees: Admission is $24 for adults and $17 for children.

Closest City or Town: Chicago

How to Get There: In Chicago, head south on S Federal St, turn right onto W Van Buren St, turn left onto S Clark St, and then continue onto East Ida B. Wells Drive. Turn right onto S Columbus Dr, turn left onto E McFetridge Dr, left onto Special Olympics Dr, make a U-turn at E Solidarity Dr, and then turn right to reach the museum at 1400 S Lake Shore Dr.

GPS Coordinates: 41.86750° N, 87.61699° W

Did You Know? The Field Museum includes a few working laboratories, with one that studies DNA extraction and another where paleontologists prepare fossils for study.

Lakefront Trail

You will experience the most beautiful views of Chicago from Lakefront Trail, an 18-mile paved trail on the Lake Michigan shoreline. The trail is open for biking, rollerblading, walking, and running. The trail goes through many beaches on Lake Michigan, including Ohio Street, Montrose, Grant Park, and South Shore beaches. You'll come across a few dining spots, plus find easy access to many attractions. Some of the places you can visit off the trail include the Museum of Science and Industry, the Navy Pier, and the Peggy Notebaert Nature Museum.

Best Time to Visit: The summer season is the best time, as more of the waterfront dining spaces on the trail are open then.

Pass/Permit/Fees: You can visit the trail for free, but it costs money to rent a bike.

Closest City or Town: Chicago

How to Get There: In Chicago, head north on S Federal St and turn right onto W Jackson Blvd. Turn left onto S Columbus Dr, right onto E Monroe St, and then turn left onto Jean Baptiste Point du Sable Lake Shore Dr/S Lake Shore Dr. Continue onto Jean Baptiste Point du Sable Lake Shore Dr/N Lake Shore Dr. Turn right onto N Sheridan Rd and right onto W Ardmore Ave to reach the northern trailhead.

GPS Coordinates: 41.04051° N, 87.65466° W

Did You Know? You can visit the trail 24 hours a day.

Lincoln Park Zoo

Lincoln Park Zoo in Chicago is one of the country's most historic zoos, founded in 1868. Lincoln Park Zoo has more than 200 species of animals on its grounds. The zoo houses many exciting habitats, including an arctic section with polar bears, camel and zebra habitats, and a penguin cover. There's also a sanctuary featuring many birds of prey like owls and vultures. The zoo has an interactive farm for children, featuring various goats, cows, rabbits, and other animals.

Best Time to Visit: The zoo offers special holiday activities in November and December.

Pass/Permit/Fees: Admission to the zoo is free, although donations are encouraged. Some features like the carousel and train require a fee.

Closest City or Town: Chicago

How to Get There: In Chicago, head north on S Federal St and turn right onto W Jackson Blvd. Turn left onto Jean Baptiste Point du Sable Lake Shore Dr/S Lake Shore Dr and then use the Lasalle Dr exit to get onto left W LaSalle Dr. Turn right onto N Stockton Dr, turn left onto W Dckens Dr, and then right onto N Lincoln Park W. There is a parking garage at 2100 N Lincoln Park W. From the parking garage, it's a three-minute walk to the zoo.

GPS Coordinates: 41.92174° N, 87.63364° W

Did You Know? The zoo features one of the oldest bur oak trees in the city. The zoo dates back to about 1830, a few years before the formation of Chicago.

Maggie Daley Park

Maggie Daley Park offers many activities for the family near the Chicago lakefront. The park features a vast garden with a pergola and columns from the demolished Federal Building dating back to 1905.

The park has a climbing wall where people can test their skills, tennis courts, an ice-skating rink, and a miniature golf course featuring holes inspired by Chicago landmarks. The Play Garden features a vast playground with fountains, slides, and other activities for children. Many of the sites here offer unique views of the Chicago skyline.

Best Time to Visit: Most of the attractions at the park are open from April to September.

Pass/Permit/Fees: It costs money to rent equipment, play on the miniature golf course, or use the climbing wall.

Closest City or Town: Chicago

How to Get There: In Chicago, head north on S Federal St and turn right onto W Jackson Blvd. Turn left onto S Columbus Dr and then turn right to reach the nearest parking garage to the park at 5 S Columbus Dr. From the parking garage, walk south and turn left onto S Columbus St and then take a left onto E Monroe St to reach the park at 337 E Randolph St. It's about a three-minute walk.

GPS Coordinates: 41.88258° N, 87.61939° W

Did You Know? The park is named for Maggie Daley, the wife of former city mayor Richard M. Daley, the son of fellow mayor Richard J. Daley.

Montrose Beach

Montrose Beach is near Chicago's Uptown neighborhood and the Chicago Park District. It offers sandy dunes, a beach house, and a dock where drinks and small meals are available. The area also features a small docking marina where visitors can rent a kayak to paddle around the water.

Montrose Beach hosts the Montrose Point Bird Sanctuary, as well as a series of fields for football and soccer, including one artificial turf field for local athletic competitions.

Best Time to Visit: The fall is a popular time, as the autumn colors will be instantly noticeable around the dunes.

Pass/Permit/Fees: The beach is free to visit, although it costs extra to rent a kayak.

Closest City or Town: Chicago

How to Get There: In Chicago, head north on S Federal St and take a right onto W Jackson Blvd. Turn left onto S Lake Shore Dr and then continue onto US-41 N/N Lake Shore Dr. Take the Montrose exit and turn right onto W Montrose Ave. Continue onto N Simonds Dr to reach the beach at 4400 N Lake Shore Dr.

GPS Coordinates: 41.96712° N, 87.63862° W

Did You Know? There is a dog-friendly stretch of beach at the northern end.

Museum of Science and Industry

The Museum of Science and Industry is one of Chicago's most famous museums. Located on Chicago's lakefront, it is housed in a building once used in the 1893 World's Columbian Exposition.

The museum holds the Apollo 8 spacecraft, a re-creation of a coal mine, a mockup of a Chicago street in the early twentieth century, and a farming exhibit. A U-505 German submarine is also on display here as well as a massive and detailed dollhouse owned by actress and investor Colleen Moore.

Best Time to Visit: The museum hosts many traveling exhibits throughout the year. Check with the museum to learn about what is appearing here before visiting.

Pass/Permit/Fees: Tickets are $21.95 for adults and $12.95 for children. It also costs extra to enter some attractions, including the U-505 and coal mine.

Closest City or Town: Chicago

How to Get There: In Chicago, head north on S Federal St and turn right onto W Jackson Blvd. Take a right onto US-41 S and stay right on US-41 S. Turn right onto Science Dr and right onto Columbia Dr to reach 5700 S Lake Shore Dr.

GPS Coordinates: 41.79074° N, 87.58309° W

Did You Know? The Boeing 727 on display at the museum is the first such 727 to have been used in commercial service. You can enter the inside of the plane.

Navy Pier

The Navy Pier is one of the most popular attractions in downtown Chicago. The pier was constructed in 1916 and features various attractions for families. Navy Pier houses boats that offer short cruises and rides along the Chicago lakefront. The pier also has an indoor botanical garden surrounded by a glass atrium, a funhouse maze attraction, and various shops and restaurants. The Chicago Children's Museum and the Chicago Shakespeare Theater also operate out of Navy Pier. The Ferris wheel is Navy Pier's most famous attraction. The wheel is nearly 200 feet tall and provides unique views of Chicago's skyline.

Best Time to Visit: The summer season is the most popular time to visit.

Pass/Permit/Fees: It is free to enter Navy Pier, but ticket prices will vary by attraction.

Closest City or Town: Chicago

How to Get There: The Navy Pier is off Grand Avenue and Illinois Street on Chicago's eastern end. Take the exit onto Lake Shore Drive, and then use the Illinois St exit toward Grand Ave to reach N Streeter Dr. Turn right onto E Grand Ave to reach the pier at 600 E Grand Ave.

GPS Coordinates: 41.89200° N, 87.60510° W

Did You Know? The entrance to Navy Pier features a statue of comedian and television star Bob Newhart. There's an empty bench next to him where people can sit for pictures.

North Avenue Beach

North Avenue Beach features a trail for walking and biking. There are a few volleyball courts to the south, plus two small dining spots near the beach. The southern end features a walkway that protrudes outward into Lake Michigan. It's a popular point for photos, as you can see much of Chicago's skyline from here.

The Chess Pavilion is on the southern part of the beach. It includes various chess-themed sculptures and boards.

Best Time to Visit: In August, North Avenue Beach is one of the best places to view the annual Chicago Air and Water Show.

Pass/Permit/Fees: The beach is free to enter, although it costs extra to rent a bike.

Closest City or Town: Chicago

How to Get There: In Chicago, head north on S Federal St, take a right onto W Jackson Blvd and use the left three lanes to follow S Lake Shore Dr. In 3.5 miles, take the Fullerton Pkwy Exit and continue until you can turn left onto N Cannon Dr to reach the beach.

GPS Coordinates: 41.91781° N, 87.62694° W

Did You Know? The Consulate General of the Republic of Poland is across from the beach.

Oak Street Beach

Oak Street Beach is near Chicago's Gold Coast neighborhood. The Chicago Park District operates the beach, which offers views of Chicago's skyline.

The beach houses a café, a few spots for beach volleyball, and various biking trails. There is also a mural dedicated to preserving the water. The mural is about 260 feet long and 9 feet high.

Best Time to Visit: The beach is popular during the summer, but visit during the Chicago Air and Water Show in August if possible. The beach offers great views of the action during the show.

Pass/Permit/Fees: The beach is free to access, but it costs extra to rent volleyball equipment or a bicycle.

Closest City or Town: Chicago

How to Get There: The beach is accessible through crossings near Bellevue Place and Division Street. The beach is also near the Clark/Division CTA Red Line station. The CTA 22, 36, and 151 bus routes also serve the area.

GPS Coordinates: 41.90315° N, 87.62285° W

Did You Know? The beach first became popular in the early twentieth century after the construction of the Chicago Drainage Canal, which prevents sewage from entering Lake Michigan.

Old Watertower

The Old Watertower is one of the oldest buildings in Chicago. The tower is symbolic of the city's rise from the Great Chicago Fire of 1871.

The tower was built in 1869 to house a water pump. It is about 180 feet in height and features an ornate stone body. It survived the Great Chicago Fire and is one of the few buildings left in the city from before that event. As part of Jane Byrne Park, it is located east of the Loyola University Chicago Water Tower Campus.

Best Time to Visit: The tower is often decorated with Christmas lights during the winter season.

Pass/Permit/Fees: You can visit the tower for free.

Closest City or Town: Chicago

How to Get There: In Chicago, head east on W Jackson Blvd, turn left onto S State St, right toward N Wabash Ave, and then left onto N Wabash Ave. Take a right onto E Chicago Ave and then a left onto E Tower Ct to reach the Old Watertower at 109 E Pearson St.

GPS Coordinates: 41.89714° N, 87.62496° W

Did You Know? The water tower is the second-oldest water tower in the country, predated by one in Louisville, Kentucky.

Shedd Aquarium

The Shedd Aquarium is one of the world's largest aquariums, located in Chicago, south of Grant Park on Lake Michigan. The Shedd Aquarium features more than 30,000 species of animals in about 5 million gallons of water. The venue features a Caribbean exhibit with schooling fish, stingrays, tarpons, and many other ocean creatures.

The Amazon section features a flooded rainforest with various reptiles, birds, and fish. The oceanarium exhibit hosts beluga whales, sea otters, and various species of penguins. There's also a stingray tank where people can touch the cownose rays as they swim.

Best Time to Visit: The aquarium is open year-round and exciting to see at any time.

Pass/Permit/Fees: Adult tickets are $39.95, while children ages 11 and under cost $29.95.

Closest City or Town: Chicago

How to Get There: In Chicago, head north on S Lake Shore Dr and turn right onto E Waldron Dr. Turn left onto Special Olympics Dr, continue straight and the aquarium is on the right at 1200 S Lake Shore Dr.

GPS Coordinates: 41.86776° N, 87.61405° W

Did You Know? The Shedd Aquarium once housed sea otters who were rescued in Alaska following the Exxon Valdez oil spill of 1989.

The 606

The 606 is a park and walking trail space in the Palmer Square neighborhood of Chicago. The 606 features 2.7 miles of elevated trail space for running and biking.

The trail is built on a former railway. The city converted the rail line into a walking and biking path in 2015. The design provides enough room for walking and catching the Chicago skyline in the background.

Best Time to Visit: Visit during the middle of the afternoon if possible. The 606 can be busy due to the path often being used for commuting purposes.

Pass/Permit/Fees: It is free to enter the 606.

Closest City or Town: Chicago

How to Get There: In Chicago, from W North Ave, head east on IL-64 E and turn left in two miles. Turn right onto W Armitage Ave and then right onto N Ridgeway to reach the 606 – West trailhead at 1805 N Ridgeway Ave.

GPS Coordinates: 41.91386° N, 87.72019° W

Did You Know? The 606 gets its name from the area's zip code prefix.

The Frederick C. Robie House

The Frederick C. Robie House is a building on the University of Chicago campus in Chicago's Hyde Park neighborhood. The home was built in 1909 and features a Prairie-style build designed by Frank Lloyd Wright. The Frederick C. Robie House has a Roman brick exterior with various horizontal lines that create a look reminiscent of the midwestern prairie. The glass windows feature a mix of clear and colored parts positioned at acute angles. The inside includes other Wright staples like geometric patterns and minimal adornments, creating a modern domestic design.

Best Time to Visit: The house is open from Thursday to Monday every year.

Pass/Permit/Fees: It costs $20 to take a tour of the house.

Closest City or Town: Chicago

How to Get There: From the west, take Exit 54 on I-90 at Guaranteed Rate Field and go east on 35th Street. Turn right on Michigan Avenue, and go a few miles before turning left on Garfield Boulevard. Merge right on Morgan Drive, then go left on 57th Street. Turn right on Kimbark Avenue and then right on 58th Street to reach 5757 S Woodlawn Ave. The nearest train station is the University of Chicago/59th Street stop on the Metra Electric Line.

GPS Coordinates: 41.78996° N, 87.59596° W

Did You Know? The Frederick Robie House is one of the many Wright homes highlighted by Lego in a brick set of nearly 2,300 pieces.

Willis Tower Skydeck

The Willis Tower was the world's tallest building when it opened in 1974. The 1,729-foot building remains one of the tallest to this day. The Skydeck is 1,353 feet above street level, providing a full view of everything in downtown Chicago. Visitors can also stand on the Ledge, a glass enclosure that stretches 4 feet outside the tower.

You'll also learn about the tower's unique bundled tube construction and how the building can handle the wind sway that occurs around the top.

Best Time to Visit: Arrive about half an hour before sunset to get a beautiful view.

Pass/Permit/Fees: Tickets start at $28 for adults and $22 for children.

Closest City or Town: Chicago

How to Get There: In Chicago, follow I-90 W and take exit 51H for I-290 W. Keep right at the fork, take Exit 51I, and follow signs for Ida B Wells Dr. Merge onto IL-110 E and take the Wacker Dr exit. Keep right at the fork and follow the signs for Upper Wacker Dr. Continue onto S Wacker Dr, turn right onto W Jackson Blvd, and access to the Skydeck is on the left at 233 S Wacker Dr.

GPS Coordinates: 41.87905° N, 87.63595° W

Did You Know? The building was originally called the Sears Tower and was the headquarters of the Sears department store until 1994.

Wrigley Field

Wrigley Field is a must-see attraction for baseball fans of all ages. Wrigley Field, built in 1914, is the home of the Chicago Cubs and one of the oldest ballparks around.

The ballpark features a distinct manually operated scoreboard in centerfield. The outfield wall is made of brick, with several ivy vines covering the entire surface. Wrigley Field tours are available. You can visit the bleachers, see the Cubs dugout, and get an up-close look at the ivy.

Best Time to Visit: Tours are available year-round if you can't get to a Cubs game.

Pass/Permit/Fees: Tours cost $30 per person. Ticket prices will vary for Cubs games.

Closest City or Town: Chicago

How to Get There: In Chicago, use W Belmont Ave to turn right onto N Lake Shore Dr. Take a left onto W Addison St and a right onto N Sheffield Ave to reach the ballfield at 1060 W Addison St.

GPS Coordinates: 41.94992° N, 87.65545° W

Did You Know? The Chicago Bears football team also played at Wrigley Field from 1921 to 1970 until they moved to Soldier Field.

White Pines Forest State Park

You'll find the White Pines Forest State Park north of the Rock River near the towns of Dixon and Oregon. The park is about 30 miles southwest of Rockford and features nearly 400 acres of terrain. It includes some of the southernmost white pine trees in the country. The Canadian yew and many other rare flowers also grow in the park.

The park is popular among birdwatching enthusiasts, as many birds travel through the area and migrate during the winter. You'll also find cross-country skiing trails in the winter and an archery range in the summer.

Best Time to Visit: The white pine trees are especially noticeable in the fall season.

Pass/Permit/Fees: You can rent a camping site for $10 per night. A site with electricity costs $20 per night.

Closest City or Town: Dixon

How to Get There: From Dixon, head west on E 6th St and then turn right onto S Galena Ave. Turn right onto Lowell Park Rd and right onto W Pines Rd. Turn left, keep left, and then take another left to reach the parking lot for White Pines Forest State Park.

GPS Coordinates: 41.99345° N, 89.46698° W

Did You Know? Fishing is not allowed here, but you can hunt for deer as part of the state's deer population reduction program. You will require a license for hunting first.

Dixon Springs State Park

Dixon Springs State Park is in Pope County in southern Illinois. The park features a massive sandstone block that was deposited here more than 300 million years ago. You will see many small canyons and waterfalls throughout the park.

The park features a few small church buildings in the middle of the area. There are also four walking trails, including the Oak Tree and Pine Tree trails, that offer beautiful views of the natural mushrooms growing throughout the park. The Ghost Dance Trail to the south offers more of a challenge for experienced hikers.

Best Time to Visit: Visit in the spring or fall, as conditions can be very humid in the summer.

Pass/Permit/Fees: You can visit the park for free, but it may cost extra to reserve a camping space here, depending on the season.

Closest City or Town: Eddyville

How to Get There: From Eddyville, head south on High St and turn left onto W Pine St. Take a slight right onto Main St, turn right onto IL-145 S. Turn left onto Franks Road, left onto IL-145 E and the park is on the left at 982 IL-146.

GPS Coordinates: 37.38111° N, 88.6663° W

Did You Know? You can collect a bird checklist from the park office when you enter the park. The checklist includes an overview of the diverse array of birds you can find while in the park.

Jon J. Duerr Forest Preserve

You will find the Jon J. Duerr Forest Preserve south of Elgin on the Fox River. The preserve features a woodland area for hiking and birdwatching. There is also a small shore space on the river where you can hold a picnic. You can also launch a boat into the Fox River on the southwestern end of the preserve.

There is a statue of Black Hawk at the entrance, a Sauk leader for whom the Black Hawk War of 1832 is named. There is also an 8-foot waterfall on the bike trail that moves directly to a small creek that goes through part of the forest.

Best Time to Visit: The morning is a great time to visit, as the area is not too busy. The spring season is also an ideal time for a visit.

Pass/Permit/Fees: Admission is free, although donations are recommended.

Closest City or Town: Elgin

How to Get There: In Elgin, head southeast on State Rte 31 N and then turn right onto Bonnie St. In 0.3 miles, turn left to reach the preserve at 35W003 State Rte 31.

GPS Coordinates: 41.97855° N, 88.29906° W

Did You Know? The preserve features a memorial dedicated to the unknown soldiers of an army led by General Winfield Scott.

Chicago Great Western Railroad Depot

The Chicago Great Western Railroad Depot is in the northwestern town of Elizabeth. The rail station was built in 1877 as part of the Chicago Great Western Railway between Chicago and Oelwein, Iowa.

The museum houses many artifacts from the railroad and the rail line. You'll also find a scale model railroad here. Some of the models are G-scale, which is one of the largest scale sizes.

You'll find the Commercial Hotel across the street from the depot. The hotel was utilized as a place for travelers to stay while on the rail line.

Best Time to Visit: The museum is open on weekends from May to October.

Pass/Permit/Fees: Admission to the museum is free. The Elizabeth Historical Society runs the venue.

Closest City or Town: Elizabeth

How to Get There: In Elizabeth, head southwest on E Myrtle St toward Madison St and the depot is on the left at 111 E Myrtle St.

GPS Coordinates: 42.31723° N, 90.22249° W

Did You Know? The depot has a distinct Stick-style construction. It features board strips laid over the front to create a look that suggests the frame is slightly exposed.

Cave-In-Rock

Cave-In-Rock is one of the most intriguing villages in the state of Illinois, located on the southern end of the state on the Ohio River in Hardin County. Cave-In-Rock was a prominent village among various outlaws in the midwestern frontier. Highwaymen and river pirates resided in Cave-In-Rock to avoid capture. Among the people who lived in the area included the Harpe brothers, Philip Alston, and the Sturdivant Gang. Permanent settlers would arrive in the area in 1816.

Cave-In-Rock is home to Cave-In-Rock State Park that features a distinct cave formed by erosion from a local bluff. The park also has various riverside spaces that were once used as ferry stations.

Best Time to Visit: The spring is a great time to visit, as temperatures can become warm in the summer.

Pass/Permit/Fees: You can visit Cave-In-Rock for free.

Closest City or Town: Elizabethtown

How to Get There: From Elizabethtown, head east on IL-146 E and turn right onto IL-1 S. Turn left onto Main St and right onto Broadway St, which turns left and becomes Park Ave. The parking lot for Cave-In-Rock State Park is on the right, and you'll pass through the village to reach it.

GPS Coordinates: 37.46969° N, 88.15696° W

Did You Know? Cave-In-Rock has one river crossing. You can take a ferry from the town to Crittenden, Kentucky.

Garden of the Gods

The Garden of the Gods is a landmass on the eastern end of the Shawnee National Forest in southern Illinois. The garden features about 3,000 acres of land scattered across four counties.

The Garden of the Gods houses many sandstone formations surrounding a quarter-mile trail. The region features many high cliffs and beautiful trees. The area also features a few camping sites near the larger Indian Point Loop hiking trail.

Best Time to Visit: The fall is a great time to visit, as the trees in the area will be flush with beautiful orange and yellow colors.

Pass/Permit/Fees: You can use a campsite for $10 per night. Up to eight people and two vehicles are allowed on a campsite. No reservations are necessary.

Closest City or Town: Equality

How to Get There: In Equality, head east on IL-13 E toward Old Hwy 13 and turn right onto State Rte 142 S. Take a right onto S Walnut St. Continue onto Shawnee Forest Rd and then onto Horseshoe Rd. Follow Forest Rd and then continue onto Co Rd 17. Take a right onto Garden of the Gods Rd, and then continue to Picnic Rd to reach the trail inside of the Shawnee National Forest.

GPS Coordinates: 37.60486° N, 88.38438° W

Did You Know? Many of the trees here are second-growth trees. These are trees that grow back after first being harvested.

Lighthouse Beach

Lighthouse Beach is on the shore of Lake Michigan, north of Northwestern University campus in Evanston. The beach is a private venue accessible only to those who pay the proper fee for entry.

Lighthouse Beach features plenty of room for picnics and other activities on the sand. The beach also houses the Grosse Point Lighthouse building and the Harley Clarke Mansion.

Best Time to Visit: The beach isn't as busy from Tuesday to Friday.

Pass/Permit/Fees: It costs $10 to access the beach between Memorial Day and Labor Day. Evanston residents can access the beach for free from Saturday to Monday.

Closest City or Town: Evanston

How to Get There: In Evanston, turn right onto Ridge Ave from Grove St, right onto Lincoln St, and left onto Sheridan Rd. Take a right and then the beach is on the left.

GPS Coordinates: 42.06501° N, 87.67493° W

Did You Know? The beach is due west of Ryan Field, the home of the Northwestern University Wildcats college football team.

Northwestern University - Lincoln St. Beach

Northwestern University – Lincoln St. Beach has a beach property available to students and the public in Evanston, north of the Ryan Fieldhouse.

This location is popular as one of the more exclusive beach sites in the Chicago area. The beach area is also open for swimming throughout most of the day, from nine in the morning to eight in the evening.

Best Time to Visit: Visit during the summer, as the campus won't be as crowded with students.

Pass/Permit/Fees: It costs $8 for adults or $6 for children to access the beach. Full-time Northwestern students and Henry Crown Sports Pavilion members can access the beach for free.

Closest City or Town: Evanston

How to Get There: In Evanston, head north and turn left onto Grove St. Turn right onto Ridge Ave and then right onto Lincoln St. Lincoln St turns into Campus Dr and the beach access is on the left.

GPS Coordinates: 42.06142° N, 87.67303° W

Did You Know? Northwestern is one of Illinois's oldest universities. It was formed in 1851.

Cahokia Mounds State Historic Site

You will find some of the earliest Native American sites in Illinois at the Cahokia Mounds State Historic Site in Collinsville, a western suburb of St. Louis, Missouri.

Cahokia Mounds includes over 2,200 acres of land. You will find 80 mounds throughout the historic site. These mounds were home to a vast Native American settlement called Cahokia, which had a population of nearly 20,000 people around the year 1100 CE.

Each mound has a unique story, with many of the mounds being home to excavation sites to help find various artifacts and remnants of the tribes that lived here. You'll see many of the items found here at the interpretive center on site.

Best Time to Visit: You can visit during the summer season when it is brighter out.

Pass/Permit/Fees: Admission is free, but donations are encouraged. Expect to spend at least $10 on donations here.

Closest City or Town: Fairmont City

How to Get There: From Fairmont City, head north on N 45th St and turn right onto Collinsville Rd. Continue straight to Cahokia Mounds State Historic Site.

GPS Coordinates: 38.65684° N, 90.06167° W

Did You Know? Monks Mound is the most prominent mound at the site at about 100 feet high and nearly 1,000 feet wide. The mound is the largest manmade mound of its type north of Mexico.

Thunder Bay Falls

The Galena Territory in the northwestern town of Galena houses Thunder Bay Falls, one of the most beautiful waterfalls in the state. The waterfall is on the southwestern end of Lake Galena.

Thunder Bay Falls is about 40 feet high and features various rock cliffs and water columns. Visitors will also see birds throughout the area, including wild turkeys, blue herons, ospreys, and even eagles.

Best Time to Visit: Visit during the spring and summer, as you'll be more likely to find various birds out here.

Pass/Permit/Fees: The waterfall is free to visit.

Closest City or Town: Galena

How to Get There: From Galena, head southwest on S Bench St and turn right to stay on S Bench St. Turn left onto US-20 E/Us Hwy 20 W. Turn left onto W Mt Hope Rd and then left onto Thunder Bay Rd to reach the falls at 233 Thunder Bay Rd.

GPS Coordinates: 42.40047° N, 90.35224° W

Did You Know? The waterfall is a small part of the Galena Territory, a community that offers a marina and various semi-private golf courses.

Abbey Farms

You'll find a quaint escape from the city at Abbey Farms in Aurora. The Monks of Marmion Abbey have been operating Abbey Farms since 1949.

Abbey Farms has a full cornfield where you can buy sweet corn and various other produce grown in the area. The farm is available for tours throughout the year.

The farms also house a small brewery and winery, producing various drinks. There is also a small live music area that offers concerts throughout the year.

Best Time to Visit: Abbey Farms hosts the Pumpkin Daze fall festival in October and the Christmas Joy festival in December. You'll find many Christmas trees for sale in December, including precut ones and ones you can cut yourself.

Pass/Permit/Fees: You can visit the farm for free, but it costs extra to partake in some activities here.

Closest City or Town: Geneva

How to Get There: From Geneva, take IL-25 S and turn left onto E Wilson St. Take a right onto S Van Buren St, left onto Pine St, and right onto Hart Rd to reach Abbey Farms on the left in 1.9 miles at 2855 Hart Rd.

GPS Coordinates: 41.82777° N, 88.30107° W

Did You Know? The wines and beer available at the farm are only available on site. You cannot buy these products online.

Cantigny Park

Cantigny Park is found in the western Chicago suburb of Wheaton. The park features 500 acres of land and a few historical sites.

Cantigny Park is home to the McCormick House, a mansion once owned by former *Chicago Tribune* publisher Robert McCormick. The 1896 mansion is adorned with many unique accents. The park also features the First Division Museum, highlighting the First Division of the United States Army. You will see a few tanks and artillery pieces outside the museum.

Best Time to Visit: Visit during the spring and summer, as the gardens are in bloom and the golf course is easier to access then.

Pass/Permit/Fees: It costs $5 to park, but it may also cost $10 during the summer or on weekends. It also costs extra to golf here.

Closest City or Town: Geneva

How to Get There: From Geneva, head northwest and turn right onto Brittany Ct. Take a right onto IL-38 E, turn right onto Winfield Rd, and then take a left to reach Cantigny Park at 1 S 151 Winfield Road.

GPS Coordinates: 41.85479° N, 88.15658° W

Did You Know? Cantigny Park is on land once owned by Joseph Medill. He was the mayor of Chicago after the Great Chicago Fire of 1871 and co-owner of the *Chicago Tribune*.

Fabyan Forest Reserve

The Fabyan Forest Reserve is in southern Geneva on the shore of the Fox River. Most of the preserve is on the western side of the river.

The preserve houses the Fabyan Villa Museum, a site featuring a farmhouse that was remodeled and expanded by Frank Lloyd Wright. You'll find many of Wright's Prairie-style architectural accents throughout the museum.

The reserve also features a 1-acre Japanese-style garden. The Gingko tree has been growing in the garden since it was first planted in 1910. There's also a Dutch windmill on the eastern end of the river. The 1870 landmark is about 68 feet high and is open for tours.

Best Time to Visit: The reserve is open from May to October.

Pass/Permit/Fees: Admission is free, but donations are suggested. Most donations are less than $10 per person.

Closest City or Town: Geneva

How to Get There: From Geneva, head onto W State St and turn right onto S Bennett St. Turn right onto Crissey Ave, right onto E Fabyan Pkwy, and then right again onto State Rte 31 N/S Batavia Ave. Take a right and then a left to reach 1925 S Batavia Ave.

GPS Coordinates: 41.86951° N, 88.31118° W

Did You Know? A small tea house is in the middle of the Japanese garden.

Bork Falls

Bork Falls is one of the most inviting swimming holes in Shawnee National Forest in southern Illinois. The waterfall is located off the trail at Ferne Cliffe State Park.

You'll find the water falling into a blue-green pool at Bork Falls that is gentle and nice for swimming. The water slides into the pool through a narrow opening over a beautiful limestone formation.

Best Time to Visit: Bork Falls is best during the summer. The rock formation provides enough shade to keep the area cool even when it gets hot.

Pass/Permit/Fees: You can visit for free, but you'll need to watch where you park.

Closest City or Town: Goreville

How to Get There: From Goreville, head north on S Broadway and turn left onto W Main St. Continue onto Goreville Rd and then turn left onto Regent Ln. The falls are on the right.

GPS Coordinates: 37.54198° N, 89.02119° W

Did You Know? Some of the rocks near the waterfall are open for climbing.

Ferne Clyffe State Park

You will find the Ferne Clyffe State Park in the Johnson County town of Goreville in southern Illinois. The park features multiple sites for picnics and camping, many offering grills and showers.

You'll find 18 trails throughout Ferne Clyffe State Park. Many of these trails surround different forest and pond spaces. You'll find moss growing on many of the natural rock formations around here, a sign of the humid conditions throughout the park.

Best Time to Visit: Conditions will not be as humid here during the fall season.

Pass/Permit/Fees: It will cost money to reserve a camping site, but you can enter the park during the day for free if you wish.

Closest City or Town: Goreville

How to Get There: From Goreville, head south on IL-37 S and take a right in 1.6 miles before making two consecutive lefts and another right to reach 90 Goreville Rd where the park is located.

GPS Coordinates: 37.53385° N, 88.98129° W

Did You Know? Some of the camping sites around the park are open to equestrians. They include places where people can tie their horses to hitching rails and troughs for water.

Apple River Canyon State Park

The Apple River Canyon State Park is near the Illinois state border with Wisconsin in Jo Daviess County. The park houses a canyon about 8.5 miles long that travels alongside the Apple River. The canyon was formed thousands of years ago as the Apple River reversed its old course and started flowing towards the Mississippi River. The canyon features a deep body with multiple hiking trails surrounding the space.

Best Time to Visit: Visit during the summer, as the weather conditions are relatively calm around this part of the state.

Pass/Permit/Fees: You can visit the canyon for free, but you must reserve a site for camping or for a picnic before arriving here.

Closest City or Town: Guilford

How to Get There: In Guilford, head southeast on W Guilford Rd and continue onto W Rawlins Rd. Turn right onto N Elizabeth Scales Mound Rd and then left onto W Menzemer Rd. In 2.2 miles, turn left onto E Stadel Rd, right onto E Schapville Rd, right onto N Scout Camp Rd, and then left onto E Townsend Rd. In 4.2 miles, turn left onto N Canyon Park Rd to reach the park at 8763 E Canyon Rd.

GPS Coordinates: 42.44767° N, 90.05299° W

Did You Know? You'll find loess throughout the Apple River Canyon, a sediment that builds up when dust is blown by the wind.

Ulysses S. Grant Home State Historic Site

You'll find the former home of President Ulysses S. Grant in the northwest Illinois town of Galena near Dubuque, Iowa. Grant lived in the home after serving in the Civil War and before becoming president. The building was constructed in 1860 and was expanded in the 1880s with a new wash house. The house has been restored to look like it did in 1868 when Grant became president. The inside features various well-defined and decorated rooms, with most of the furniture having originally belonged to Grant and his family. The dining room features many paintings of the Grant family, while the grand sitting room features a piano.

Best Time to Visit: The house is open from Wednesday to Sunday.

Pass/Permit/Fees: Admission is $5 for adults and $3 for children.

Closest City or Town: Guilford

How to Get There: From Guilford, head northwest on W Guilford Rd and turn left onto Thunder Bay Rd. Turn right onto W Mt Hope Rd and then right onto US-20 W. Turn right onto Bouthillier St, and the home is on the right at 500 Bouthillier St.

GPS Coordinates: 42.41797° N, 90.42452° W

Did You Know? Residents in the town of Galena gave Grant the house as a gift for his service in the Civil War.

Burden Falls

Burden Falls is on the southern end of Burden Creek in the Shawnee National Forest. You'll find the waterfall at the western end of the forest.

Burden Falls flows mainly during the spring and summer seasons. The water falls 20 feet and continues another 80 feet through a few cascades. The waterfall's unique shape comes from natural erosion. Visitors will find many naturally formed stones throughout the waterfall path.

Best Time to Visit: The spring and summer seasons are the best times to visit, as the waterfall may be dormant during the fall and winter.

Pass/Permit/Fees: You can visit the waterfall for free.

Closest City or Town: Harrisburg

How to Get There: From Harrisburg, head east on Old State Rte 13/W Poplar St toward N Main St. Turn right onto US-45 N/S Commercial St. Take a left onto IL-145 S/IL-34 S and continue for 11.1 miles. Turn right onto Burden Falls Rd and continue until you reach the falls on the right.

GPS Coordinates: 37.56516° N, 88.64234° W

Did You Know? Unlike many other waterfalls in the state, Burden Falls wasn't impacted by glaciation during the Ice Age.

Kankakee River State Park

The Kankakee River travels south of Chicago into the nearby cities of Kankakee, Bradley, and Bourbonnais. You'll find the Kankakee River State Park in the northwestern end of those cities.

The Kankakee River State Park features a full campground with two cabins. You can rent one of these cabins for an evening if you wish. There is also an equestrian campground open during parts of the year, offering space to secure horses overnight.

Best Time to Visit: Visit during the spring or summer, as most of the camping activities in the area are open during those seasons.

Pass/Permit/Fees: The cost to reserve a campsite or other feature at the park will vary. Check with the campsite for details on what is open here.

Closest City or Town: Kankakee

How to Get There: From Kankakee, head northwest on IL-102 W toward 3000 W Rd to reach the park at 5314 IL-102. The main entrance is near Rock Creek, but parking is also available to the west near the County Road West 700 bridge.

GPS Coordinates: 41.20822° N, 88.01327° W

Did You Know? The state park is on land that was once occupied by the Council of Three Fires, a group that included the Potawatomi, Chippewa, and Ottawa tribes.

Lake Bluff Beach

Lake Bluff Beach hosts one of the most appealing beaches in the Chicagoland area. The beach is also near a winery, golf course, and a small naval station.

Lake Bluff Beach has a beach with a rocky surface near the water. You'll find a few sandy spots closer inland, but the best area here is near the south. You'll find some open sand spaces that directly surround the water. The area is also suitable for launching a yacht or other vessel.

Best Time to Visit: The summer is the best time to sail Lake Bluff Beach.

Pass/Permit/Fees: The beach is free to visit, but you may need to reserve time to get your vessel out on the water. Check with the city for details on what's open.

Closest City or Town: Lake Forest

How to Get There: From Lake Forest, head south on Griffith Rd and turn left onto E Woodland Rd. Take a left onto N Sheridan Rd, continue straight onto Moffett Rd and turn right to stay on Moffett Rd. Turn right onto E Center Ave, left onto Sunrise Ave, and then take a sharp right to reach the beach at 784 E Prospect Ave.

GPS Coordinates: 42.27759° N, 87.82874° W

Did You Know? The Naval Station Great Lakes is to the north. It's the only boot camp run by the United States Navy.

Lake Shelbyville

An exciting part of Central Illinois, Lake Shelbyville features 11,000 acres of water surrounded by a 23,000-acre park. Lake Shelbyville borders the Wolf Creek and Eagle Creek state parks.

Much of Lake Shelbyville is formed by a dam managed by the Army Corps of Engineers. The dam produces a lake that is about 20 feet deep on average.

Lake Shelbyville features various camping and picnic sites, along with fishing, boating, horseback riding, and hiking activities. There is also an 18-hole golf course in the central part of the lake, which is located in Eagle Creek State Park.

Best Time to Visit: The spring and summer are the best times to visit.

Pass/Permit/Fees: It is free to visit the lake, but it may cost extra to camp here or rent a space for activities.

Closest City or Town: Mattoon

How to Get There: From I-57, take the East County Road 1000 North exit northeast of Mattoon and go a few miles west. You'll turn left on 2200 East Shelby County Road near Findlay.

GPS Coordinates: 39.51574° N, 88.70827° W

Did You Know? The deepest parts of the lake are close to 70 feet deep, providing enough depth for fishing.

Jackson Falls

Jackson Falls is in the middle of the Shawnee National Forest in between the towns of Ozark and Eddyville.

Jackson Falls features room for rock climbing and multiple climbing routes throughout the area. Many provide beautiful views of the nearby waterfall.

You'll see high bluffs throughout Jackson Falls, some surrounding a waterfall that drops about 20 feet. The waterfall is active throughout most of the year.

Best Time to Visit: You'll be more likely to see water flowing from the waterfall in the spring or summer.

Pass/Permit/Fees: You can camp in the area for free for up to 14 days.

Closest City or Town: Marion

How to Get There: From Marion, head east on IL-166 and turn right onto US-45 S. In 2.7 miles, turn left onto Ozark Road, and then turn right to stay on Ozark Road. Turn right onto Glen St Falls Rd, and the falls are on the right in 2.1 miles.

GPS Coordinates: 37.51468° N, 88.68415° W

Did You Know?
The park features various spots for finding wildlife—including deer, groundhogs, squirrels, and raccoons—throughout the area during most of the year.

Mississippi Palisades State Park

The Mississippi Palisades State Park in northwestern Illinois is on Buffalo Lake near the Mississippi River. The park has about 2,500 acres of land, many of which were once occupied by Native Americans.

There are 11 hiking trails throughout the park, with the longest being slightly under 2 miles. There are also a few campground sites in the middle of the park. A small creek runs through the northern part of the park.

Best Time to Visit: The park is open throughout the year.

Pass/Permit/Fees: It is free to visit the park, but you might have to reserve a camping site before your arrival. You can also play at the golf course to the northwest, but it costs extra based on the season.

Closest City or Town: Mount Carroll

How to Get There: From Mount Carroll, head east on E Benton St and turn right onto S Clay St. Turn right onto US-52 W and follow for 10.9 miles which will turn into IL-84 N/N Main St. In 2.9 miles, turn right onto Marina Rd. Take a left and then a right to reach the park at 16327A IL-84.

GPS Coordinates: 42.14405° N, 90.15381° W

Did You Know? The area was popular among Native Americans hundreds of years ago. It is believed that the easier environment and less-challenging terrain made it a useful place for them to live.

Rend Lake

You can swim, fish, or boat on Rend Lake in Jefferson and Franklin counties in southern Illinois. The lake is south of Mount Vernon and north of the Shawnee National Forest.

Rend Lake has nearly 19,000 acres of water, featuring a beach on its southern end and marinas and staging areas on the southern and central parts.

Rend Lake is a popular site for fishing. You can find various types of catfish, including the blue and flathead catfish.

Best Time to Visit: The spring is a good time to visit, as the climate is moderate here.

Pass/Permit/Fees: You can enter Rend Lake for free.

Closest City or Town: Mount Vernon

How to Get There: From Mount Vernon, head east on Broadway St and then turn right onto S 9th St. Take a right onto Jordan St and a left onto IL-37 S. Turn right onto E Franklin Road. Take a left and then a right to reach the lake.

GPS Coordinates: 38.12230° N, 88.96981° W

Did You Know? The Army Corps of Engineers formed Rend Lake in 1962. The group built a dam on the Big Muddy River to create the lake, although it did not become completely filled until 1973.

Kinkaid Lake Spillway

The end part of the Kinkaid Lake near the Big Muddy River in the Shawnee National Forest is home to the Kinkaid Lake Spillway, one of the most unique swimming holes in the state.

The spillway features a three-level cascade where people can relax and enjoy the fresh waters as they flow down.

Best Time to Visit: The spillway is more likely to have flowing water in the spring or summer, so visit the area during that time for the best experience.

Pass/Permit/Fees: It is free to get to the spillway.

Closest City or Town: Murphysboro

How to Get There: From Murphysboro, head south on N 11th St and turn right onto IL-149 W/Walnut St. In 6.9 miles, turn right onto Spillway Rd and then turn right onto N Spillway Rd to reach the spillway in the Shawnee National Forest at 432 N Spillway Rd.

GPS Coordinates: 37.77439° N, 89.45121° W

Did You Know? Be sure to wear secure sandals that can handle slippery surfaces. The rock area can get very tough to traverse after it rains.

Benedetti-Wehrli Stadium

You can watch various sports at Benedetti-Wehrli Stadium in Naperville on the North Central College campus. The venue seats 5,500 people and hosts many entertaining events each year.

The primary team at the stadium is the North Central Cardinals football team. The team competes at the Division III level of college football. The venue also hosts different college events throughout the year, plus ultimate Frisbee competitions and long-distance running events, including annual half-marathons.

Best Time to Visit: The stadium hosts a drum corps show every summer. The show highlights various drumming groups competing to be the best.

Pass/Permit/Fees: The cost to enter will vary by event.

Closest City or Town: Naperville

How to Get There: In Naperville, use I-355 S to get onto 63rd St via exit 17. Continue onto Hobson Rd and turn right onto S Naper Blvd. Turn left onto Gartner Rd, right onto Charles Ave, left onto Prairie Ave, right onto S Loomis St, and then left onto E Porter Ave to reach the stadium at 455 S Brainard St.

GPS Coordinates: 41.76957° N, 88.14595° W

Did You Know? The Chicago Fire professional soccer team played at the stadium from 2002 to 2003.

Bright Side Theatre

The Bright Side Theatre is a performing arts center on the northern end of the North Central College campus in Naperville. The theater houses many stage performances throughout the year. These include some junior versions of many prominent Broadway shows. The theater hosts classes surrounding theater and the arts throughout the year. Students can learn about acting principles and other performance factors and how to operate a stage production. The venue focuses on being a training site for people who want to enter the theater industry.

Best Time to Visit: The theater offers different shows, traditionally four in a season, with a unique theme linking them together. Check with the theater to see what is playing before you visit.

Pass/Permit/Fees: Ticket prices will vary by show.

Closest City or Town: Naperville

How to Get There: In Naperville, head west on E Ogden Ave, turn left onto N Washington St, turn left onto E Benton Ave and then take a right onto E Benton Ave. Turn right and then the parking lot for the theatre will be on the left.

GPS Coordinates: 41.77452° N, 88.14554° W

Did You Know? Many of the plays here are based on Disney shows. The Walt Disney Company supports various junior-oriented versions of its shows for younger performers.

Centennial Beach

Centennial Beach is inside a former quarry in Naperville near the DuPage River. Centennial Beach is a vast swimming hole that offers depths of up to 15 feet. The beach features various barriers for people to use when swimming, as well as a sprinkler area, a small wading spot for children, and a few diving boards.

Best Time to Visit: The beach is open from June to August, offering adult swimming hours on weekends before 11 a.m., which is when the beach opens to the rest of the public.

Pass/Permit/Fees: Daily admission is $14 for adults and $12 for children. Naperville residents can save $5 on admission. You can also enter for $6 after 5 p.m.

Closest City or Town: Naperville

How to Get There: In Naperville, head northwest on Alder Ln and then take a left onto Cypress Dr. Turn right onto Emerald Dr, right onto S West St, right onto Aurora Ave, and then left onto S Eagle St. Take a left onto Jackson Ave, another left at S West St, and then a slight right to reach the parking lot on 670W Jackson Ave, which is the closest parking to Centennial Park where the beach is located.

GPS Coordinates: 41.77161° N, 88.15758° W

Did You Know? The beach has a grill that offers various foods and desserts.

Commander Dan Shanower September 11 Memorial

Naperville was one of the first cities in the United States to have a memorial dedicated to the people who died in the September 11 terror attacks. The Commander Dan Shanower September 11 Memorial is between the city's Municipal Center and the southern bank of the DuPage River. The memorial includes a wall featuring more than 140 faces of children from the Naperville area. The memorial also incorporates about 100 pounds of rubble from the Pentagon, the building where Shanower, a Naperville native, died during the attack. A small portion of a steel beam from the World Trade Center and granite from the Flight 93 crash site in Pennsylvania is also part of the memorial, as is an outline of Shanower's boot print.

Best Time to Visit: The memorial hosts a ceremony on September 11 of each year.

Pass/Permit/Fees: The memorial is open for free throughout the year.

Closest City or Town: Naperville

How to Get There: The memorial is near the southern side of the Naperville Riverwalk. Take Eagle Street or Webster Street from the south to reach the memorial.

GPS Coordinates: 41.77135° N, 88.15166° W

Did You Know? A perennial garden surrounds the base of the memorial site.

DuPage Children's Museum

The DuPage Children's Museum in Naperville has been entertaining children in the DuPage County area for nearly 30 years. The museum offers many hands-on learning activities and hosts exhibits for preschool and elementary students. There is also a play area for children ages two and under.

While here, children can learn about science, including how shadows are formed, how energy is produced, and how physics helps objects move. There is also an art studio where children can create their own little masterpieces.

Best Time to Visit: The museum is open from Wednesday to Sunday.

Pass/Permit/Fees: Admission is $15 per person regardless of age.

Closest City or Town: Naperville

How to Get There: In Naperville, head southeast on Alder Ln and turn left onto Gartner Rd. Turn left onto Laurel Ln, right onto Sycamore Dr, and left onto S Washington St. Turn left and the museum is on the left at 301 N Washington St.

GPS Coordinates: 41.77878° N, 88.14815° W

Did You Know? The museum is one of the most inclusive in the state, as it offers a sensory-friendly experience. Service animals are welcome, and the food services at the museum can cater to various allergies and dietary needs.

First Division Museum

The First Division Museum is inside Cantigny Park in Wheaton. The museum explores the history of the First Division of the United States Army and its involvement in both world wars and the Vietnam War. You will see many authentic uniforms on display here.

The tank park houses tanks used by the Army, including Patton and Abrams models. You'll also find many old military vehicles on display, including one military truck dating back to 1918.

Best Time to Visit: Visit during the summer, as many of the military vehicles will hit the road as part of various parades at Cantigny Park.

Pass/Permit/Fees: It is free to visit, but parking costs $10.

Closest City or Town: Naperville

How to Get There: From Naperville, head northwest on Alder Ln and take a left onto Cypress Dr. Turn right onto Emerald Dr, right onto S West St, right onto Aurora Ave, left onto S Eagle St, left onto Jackson Ave, right onto S Mill St, and then continue onto Warrenville Rd. Take a right onto Winfield Rd and then turn right to reach the park at 1s151 Winfield Rd.

GPS Coordinates: 41.85266° N, 88.15532° W

Did You Know? The First Division has participated in almost every American war since its formation in 1917, making it the oldest continuously serving division in the Army.

Knoch Knolls Nature Center

You will find many spaces for fishing at the Knoch Knolls Nature Center in Naperville. Knoch Knolls features a boat launch area for small boats and kayaks. You can access one of the local trails for fishing from the boat launch site.

The center also features five bridges, with a few offering room for fishing. You'll also find two picnic areas and an 18-hole disc golf course at the park.

Best Time to Visit: The spring is a good time to visit, as the conditions will not be as humid during that season. You can purchase discs for the disc golf course at the center.

Pass/Permit/Fees: Admission is free, but you must obtain a fishing license in DuPage County if you want to fish here.

Closest City or Town: Naperville

How to Get There: From Naperville, head southeast on Alder Ln and turn left onto Gartner Rd. Turn right onto S Washington St, turn right onto Ring Rd, and left onto Knoch Knolls Rd to reach the nature center at 320 Knoch Knolls Rd.

GPS Coordinates: 41.71650° N, 88.14150° W

Did You Know? The reserve features about 5.5 miles of walking trails that offer views of various local plants and trees.

Millennium Wall

The Millennium Wall park is located near Quarry Lake and DuPage River. It is part of the Naperville Riverwalk, a site that's home to a small beach space, a sledding hill for the winter, and a skate park for the summer. The Millennium Wall features several tiers of grass fields surrounding a stone wall. The names on the wall list many people and businesses who supported its construction in 2000. The wall is near the Millennium Carillon, a 16-story observation tower with a 72-bell music system. The top of the tower features views of Naperville and its surrounding areas.

Best Time to Visit: Visit during a clear day if possible. You can see downtown Chicago from the top of the carillon when it is clear outside.

Pass/Permit/Fees: It costs $3 to travel to the top of the carillon.

Closest City or Town: Naperville

How to Get There: From Naperville, merge onto I-355 N and take exit 20 onto I-88 E toward Chicago. Continue straight to stay on I-88 E. Merge onto I-290 E and continue onto IL-110 E. Keep left on W Ida B. Wells Dr and then left onto E Congress Plaza Dr. Turn right onto S Michigan Ave and right onto E Monroe St to reach 201 E Randolph St. Be prepared to pay tolls.

GPS Coordinates: 41.77001° N, 88.15678° W

Did You Know? The Millennium Wall is near the Naper Settlement, a re-creation of a pioneer village.

Naper Settlement

The Naper Settlement highlights the Naperville area around the time of the city's formation. It houses many outdoor exhibits and includes nearly 30 buildings.

You will see exhibits surrounding blacksmithing, cooking, firefighting, and education in the nineteenth century. The houses are well preserved and feature many authentic materials from this era. The settlement also hosts various events during the year, such as summer concerts and an annual Civil War reenactment program.

Best Time to Visit: The Naper Settlement has a full calendar featuring various events. Check with the settlement to see what new events are coming to the area.

Pass/Permit/Fees: Adults can enter for $12, while children will cost $8.

Closest City or Town: Naperville

How to Get There: From Naperville, head northwest on Alder Ln and turn left onto Cypress Dr. Turn right onto Emerald Dr, right onto S West St, and then right onto Aurora Ave to reach the settlement at 523 S Webster St on the right.

GPS Coordinates: 41.76989° N, 88.15166° W

Did You Know? The settlement is part of the Blue Star Museums program. Active duty military members and their immediate families can enter for free.

Naperville Century Walk

The Naperville Century Walk is a unique tribute to Naperville's extensive history. The downtown walkway features 50 public art pieces.

The Century Walk's main highlight is the Great Concerto mural outside the Naperville Community Concert Center building. The walkway also includes many other murals highlighting Naperville's history, from its early settlement to its evolution in the twentieth century.

You'll also find many appealing statues along the walkway, including some dedicated to local heroes and volunteers, plus a statue of settler Joe Naper.

Best Time to Visit: The Century Walk is open throughout the year.

Pass/Permit/Fees: It is free to visit the Century Walk.

Closest City or Town: Naperville

How to Get There: The Century Walk starts near the DuPage River and the Naperville Riverwalk. Take Maple Avenue west off of I-355 to reach downtown. Maple Avenue becomes East Chicago Avenue after you pass Benedictine University.

GPS Coordinates: 41.77246° N, 88.14878° W

Did You Know? One of the statues here is of the famed comic strip detective Dick Tracy. Longtime Naperville resident Dick Locher worked on the strip for years and was a cartoonist for the *Chicago Tribune*.

Naperville Community Concert Center

The Naperville Community Concert Center hosts various public arts performances throughout the year. The venue is outdoors and features a massive mural called the Great Concerto on the exterior wall. The wall opens to reveal a performance stage overlooking several rows of outside seating.

The Naperville Municipal Band performs concerts throughout the year. Other local community performing arts entities also hold shows at the center. The venue focuses mainly on classical music performances.

Best Time to Visit: Most of the events occur during the summer.

Pass/Permit/Fees: The shows at the center are free.

Closest City or Town: Naperville

How to Get There: The center is on Central Park Road in downtown Naperville. To reach the venue, go west on Maple Avenue and East Chicago Avenue off of I-355. The Naperville stop on the BNSF Metra train line is five blocks north and goes between Aurora and Chicago's Union Station.

GPS Coordinates: 41.77392° N, 88.14667° W

Did You Know? Many of the events are sponsored by North Central College, a school to the southeast of the center.

Naperville Riverwalk

You will find many leisurely activities on the Naperville Riverwalk. The walkway, comprised of about 1.75 miles of brick, is on both sides of the DuPage River.

The Riverwalk features a covered bridge in the middle. The north end of the river features Centennial Beach, a small inland beach recreation area with a picnic spot, skate park, playground, and various gardens.

The south end features a café, various trees along the walkways, and the Millennium Carillon. The carillon overlooks the city with an observation deck at the top.

Best Time to Visit: Visit during clear days, as you can see downtown Chicago from the top of the carillon.

Pass/Permit/Fees: It is free to enter the Riverwalk, but additional fees apply for rentals, food, and carillon access.

Closest City or Town: Naperville

How to Get There: In Naperville, head northwest on Alder Ln, turn left onto Cypress, right onto Emerald, and then take another right onto S West St. Turn right onto Aurora Ave, and then take two consecutive lefts to reach the Naperville Riverwalk.

GPS Coordinates: 41.77044° N, 88.15649° W

Did You Know? The Riverwalk was built in 1981 to honor the city's 150th anniversary.

Paddleboat Quarry

Paddleboat Quarry is next to the Naperville Riverwalk. You can rent a paddleboat for up to four people in Quarry Lake, head out on a paddleboard, or opt for a one or two-person kayak.

Quarry Lake features beautiful trees that line Riverwalk Park on the southern end of the DuPage River. The venue offers a fun and peaceful escape from the bustle of the Chicagoland area.

Best Time to Visit: The quarry is open from the spring to fall, but the venue will close when air temperatures are under 65 degrees. Before Memorial Day and after August, this attraction is only open on the weekends.

Pass/Permit/Fees: It costs $12 to rent a paddleboat or $10 to rent a paddleboard for 20 minutes. A one-person kayak costs $10 for 20 minutes. You can add an additional 20 minutes to any of these for $5.

Closest City or Town: Naperville

How to Get There: In Naperville, head southeast on Alder Ln and turn left onto Garner Rd. Turn left onto Laurel Ln, right onto Sycamore Dr, and left onto S Washington St. In one mile take a left, and then two consecutive rights to reach the Paddleboat Quarry at 441 Aurora Ave.

GPS Coordinates: 41.77065° N, 88.15531° W

Did You Know? Quarry Lake is about 40 acres in size, giving you plenty of space to explore during your time here.

Solemn Oath Brewery

The Solemn Oath Brewery in Naperville is one of the most popular microbreweries in Illinois. The brewery offers various beers prepared in Naperville and focuses mainly on India Pale Ales. Some of the most popular beers at Solemn Oath are IPAs, including the Unholy Goat, End All, Butterfly Flashmob, and 50,000 Comments by Midnight.

The group also makes hazy pale ales, alcoholic seltzers, and barrel-aged beers. The place sells all of these barrels in flights, bottles, cans, and even a few in kegs.

Best Time to Visit: Visit during the evening hours, as the latest beer deliveries will be ready by then.

Pass/Permit/Fees: Costs vary depending on your beer of choice.

Closest City or Town: Naperville

How to Get There: In Naperville, take US-34 from the east or west and then turn onto W Ogden Ave. Turn left to stay on W Ogden Ave, take a right onto Quincy Ave, and then two consecutive rights to reach the brewery at 1661 Quincy Ave #179.

GPS Coordinates: 41.80178° N, 88.18957° W

Did You Know? While the brewery doesn't make food, it does invite food trucks throughout the week.

Waterfall Glen Forest Preserve

The Waterfall Glen Forest Preserve is in Lemont in DuPage County. The preserve surrounds the Argonne National Laboratory and houses about 11 miles of hiking trails. Many of the trails are open for hiking, biking, and horseback riding. People can also go cross-country skiing on the trails during the winter.

The park features various quarries and still water where you can go fishing. The southwestern end of the preserve also features an area to fly model airplanes.

Best Time to Visit: Most of the trails are surrounded by trees, so arrive in the early fall to see the unique orange and yellow hues of the fall season come to life at the preserve.

Pass/Permit/Fees: It is free to visit the preserve, but the park does not provide rentals for horses, bikes, or other things for travel around the area. You must also have a fishing license in Illinois if you want to fish here.

Closest City or Town: Naperville

How to Get There: From Naperville, take 75th Street east to I-355 S. Use exit 12B to get onto I-55 N toward Chicago and then exit 273A to reach S Cass Ave. Turn right onto Northgate Rd and then take another right. The preserve is on the left.

GPS Coordinates: 41.72531° N, 87.97341° W

Did You Know? The Argonne National Laboratory in the middle of the area was once used to develop nuclear reactors for the Manhattan Project.

Wentz Concert Hall

The Wentz Concert Hall and Fine Arts Center, on the North Central College campus in Naperville, opened in 2008 and features room for 600 patrons. The hall hosts various shows throughout the year with a focus on classical and jazz music. The Chicago Symphony Orchestra has performed here in the past.

The hall features a unique acoustics system with sound-absorbing curtains that can be adjusted to fit the needs of the stage. There are also sound chambers on the sides of the stage to let the sound bounce off of multiple surfaces as it makes its way towards the whole audience.

Best Time to Visit: Most concerts at the hall occur during the North Central College academic year.

Pass/Permit/Fees: The prices to enter will vary depending on which show you attend.

Closest City or Town: Naperville

How to Get There: In Naperville, turn right onto Maple Ave off of Cascade Dr and continue onto E Chicago Ave. Turn right onto S Brainard St, left onto E Jefferson Ave, and tthen left onto S Ellsworth St. The Wentz Concert Hall is on the right at 171 E Chicago Ave.

GPS Coordinates: 41.77254° N, 88.14554° W

Did You Know? The acoustics system at the hall was designed by the same people who created a similar system for Chicago's Pritzker Pavilion at Millennium Park.

Worth Waterfalls

The village of Worth in Cook County is home to Altman Park, located on the north bank of the Little Calumet River. The park is home to a waterfall and a manmade bridge. Worth Waterfalls features multiple paths where the water moves into the river.

The waterfalls are near a recreation site featuring an 18-hole golf course and a boat-launching ramp. You can get good views of the waterfalls from many of these places.

Best Time to Visit: Visit during the summer, as it is easier to find space to travel during that season.

Pass/Permit/Fees: You can visit the park and the waterfall for free, but it costs $10 to use the boat-launching ramp. The cost to golf at the nearby course will also vary during the year.

Closest City or Town: Oak Lawn

How to Get There: From Oak Lawn, head west on W 95th St and turn left onto S Central Ave. Take a right onto W 115th St, left onto S Ridgeland Ave, turn right onto W College Dr, and right onto IL-43 N/S Harlem Ave to reach the recreation area at 11600-, 11798 S Harlem Ave.

GPS Coordinates: 41.68062° N, 87.80348° W

Did You Know? The waterfalls are in the town of Worth, a community with one of the Chicago area's largest German and Irish populations.

Cascade Falls

Cascade Falls is in Matthiessen State Park near Oglesby, south of the Illinois River.

Cascade Falls is in a canyon with sandstone cliffs up to 100 feet high. The waterfall drops 45 feet before deflecting off of the sandstone and into the water.

You'll also notice a distinct amphitheater effect produced by the nearby stream. The walls around the space overhang the gorge, causing a unique echoing sound.

Best Time to Visit: The waterfall looks beautiful even when there isn't any water flowing out of it, so you could visit this waterfall at any time of the year if you wish.

Pass/Permit/Fees: You can visit the waterfall for free.

Closest City or Town: Oglesby

How to Get There: From Oglesby, head east on E Walnut St and turn left onto Co Hwy 23. Take a right onto IL-71 E and then another right onto IL-178 S. Turn right onto N 25th Rd to reach the falls.

GPS Coordinates: 41.29699° N, 89.02774° W

Did You Know? You'll find a small dam near the waterfall at a nearby gorge. Details on whether the dam was natural or man-made are unclear.

Giant's Bathtub Falls

You will find the Giant's Bathtub Falls in the middle of the Matthiessen State Park south of the Illinois River. The waterfall is in the northern part of the park on the Cedar Point trail south of the bridge and dam, near the local private golf course.

The waterfall goes downstream from Lake Falls. The wall features wooden stairs and round stone steps surrounding a vast stream bed. The area is noted for a flat body with plenty of small drops of water.

Best Time to Visit: Visit during the spring or fall when the humidity is not as intense.

Pass/Permit/Fees: You can visit the park for free, but it does cost extra to rent a camping site or various equipment for different activities here.

Closest City or Town: Oglesby

How to Get There: From Oglesby, head east on E Walnut St and turn left onto Co Hwy 23. Turn right onto IL-71 E, right onto IL-178 S, and then turn right onto N 25th Rd to reach the park at 2500 IL-178.

GPS Coordinates: 41.30243° N, 89.02548° W

Did You Know? The surface around the waterfall can be very damp. Be sure to wear water shoes if you visit this place.

Matthiessen State Park

Matthiessen State Park is on the east bank of the Vermillion River and is a few miles south of the Illinois River. The park has 1,700 acres of land to explore, featuring the Matthiessen Lake Waterfall, a fall that leads to a small canyon area. The area also offers more than 3 miles of hiking paths and a trail for horseback riding in the park.

You'll find an archery range and a private golf course at the northern end of the park. There's also an open field in the south for flying model planes.

Best Time to Visit: The spring and fall are the best times to visit the park.

Pass/Permit/Fees: Entrance to the park is free, but it may cost extra to rent equipment.

Closest City or Town: Oglesby

How to Get There: From Oglesby, head east on E Walnut St and turn left onto Co Hwy 23. Turn right onto IL-71 E and then right onto IL-178 S. In one mile, turn right onto N 25th Rd to reach the park at 2500 IL-178.

GPS Coordinates: 41.28255° N, 89.02413° W

Did You Know? White-tailed deer are prevalent in many parts of the park.

Starved Rock State Park

Starved Rock State Park is on the southern end of the Illinois River near Peru and Ottawa. Starved Rock houses sandstone canyons and waterfalls that were formed by the melting of glaciers thousands of years ago. Visitors can also see the Starved Rock Dam and the nearby river from the Lover's Leap Overlook or the Eagle Cliff Overlook.

The park features various hiking trails and camping areas. Fishing is available in the western end. You can also rent a kayak while at the park.

Best Time to Visit: The summer season is the best time for kayaking or hiking.

Pass/Permit/Fees: The park is free to access, although it costs extra to rent a kayak or reserve a camping site.

Closest City or Town: Oglesby

How to Get There: From Oglesby, head east on E Walnut St and turn left onto Co Hwy 23. Take a right onto IL-71 E and a left onto IL-178 N. The park is on the right at 2678 E 875th Rd.

GPS Coordinates: 41.31945° N, 89.00598° W

Did You Know? You'll find protected bald eagle habitats in various parts of the park.

Wildcat Canyon Falls

Wildcat Canyon Falls is a small portion of the Starved Rock State Park south of the Illinois River. The waterfall is the tallest in the park at about 70 feet. It is also the deepest canyon in the park at about 90 feet.

You will find two overlooks and a few climbing areas at the top part of the waterfall, including an ice-climbing section that's open during the winter. You'll also find various birds throughout the year at the waterfall, including Cape May warblers, Tennessee warblers, and many other migratory birds in the summer. House and tree sparrows can also be found here throughout the year.

Best Time to Visit: Visit during the spring, as snakes aren't as likely to appear at this time. The snakes here are safe and nonvenomous, but they may be bothersome to some people.

Pass/Permit/Fees: It is free to visit the waterfall.

Closest City or Town: Oglesby

How to Get There: From Oglesby, head east on E Walnut St and turn left onto Co Hwy 23. Take a right onto IL-71 E, turn left onto E 875th Rd, right onto Lodge Ln, and then take two consecutive lefts to reach the closest parking lot to Wildcat Canyon Falls at 2668 E 875th Rd.

GPS Coordinates: 41.31369° N, 88.96568° W

Did You Know? The trail surface near the waterfall is significantly cooler than it is in other parts of the park.

Odyssey Fun World

Odyssey Fun World in Tinley Park is an amusement area featuring a full assortment of indoor and outdoor activities.

Odyssey Fun World offers two go-kart tracks, batting cages, bumper boats, two miniature golf courses, and an inflatable obstacle course. The indoor area includes electric bumper cars and a laser tag area.

The arcade section features hundreds of games, and the park also has a café that serves pizza, sandwiches, and drinks.

Best Time to Visit: The venue isn't as busy on weekdays, so try coming out then.

Pass/Permit/Fees: Prices will vary by attraction. A 4-hour outdoor play wristband costs $25 per person and offers unlimited go-karting, golfing, and batting.

Closest City or Town: Orland Park

How to Get There: From Orland Park, head south on US-45 S and merge onto I-80 E via the ramp to Indiana. Take exit 148A and merge onto IL-43 S/S Harlem Ave. Turn left onto Oak Park Ave to reach 19111 Oak Park Ave.

GPS Coordinates: 41.54129° N, 87.78763° W

Did You Know? The park is across from the Hollywood Casino Amphitheatre, a massive outdoor concert venue that hosts prominent concerts in the spring and summer.

Buffalo Rock State Park

Buffalo Rock State Park is north of the Illinois River and west of Ottawa. The park has about 300 acres of land to explore.

Buffalo Rock is on a bluff that used to be an island in the Illinois River. The area offers various picnic and camping sites, with each camp station featuring a fire ring. There is a walking path alongside the Illinois River and two American bison living in the state park.

Best Time to Visit: The spring is a great time to visit, as the weather will be calm during that season.

Pass/Permit/Fees: You can visit the park for free, but you must get a reservation for a camping site if you want to camp here.

Closest City or Town: Ottawa

How to Get There: From Ottawa, head south on La Salle St and then turn left onto Lincoln Pl. Turn left onto Columbus St, left onto W Main St, left onto Clay St, and then right onto Ottawa Ave. Continue onto N 27th Rd/Dee Bennett Rd to reach the park at 1300 N 27th Rd.

GPS Coordinates: 41.32677° N, 88.91752° W

Did You Know? Explorer Louis Joliet and missionary Jacques Marquette both traveled through the area in 1673. The Illinois tribe also resided here until a war with the Iroquois tribe.

Glencoe Beach

You'll find Glencoe Beach north of Chicago and Evanston. Glencoe Beach features a beach house that offers locker rooms, rentals, and vending machines. The beach also includes a playground for children, spaces for beach volleyball, and interactive water features.

You can rent a kayak, sailboat, or standup paddleboard during the beach season. There are also lessons available for people to learn how to use these vessels on the water.

Best Time to Visit: The beach season is from June to early September.

Pass/Permit/Fees: Daily admission is $20 per person, while Glencoe residents receive a discount of $10. You must purchase your ticket online before arriving here. It also costs extra to rent equipment for activities.

Closest City or Town: Skokie

How to Get There: From Skokie, head north on I-94 W and use exit 30B to merge onto Dundee Rd. Turn right onto Green Bay Rd, turn left onto Park Ave, and then take a sharp left onto Hazel Ave to reach Glencoe Beach on the right at 160 Hazel Ave.

GPS Coordinates: 42.13847° N, 87.74881° W

Did You Know? Dogs are allowed on the beach during the offseason, but you cannot bring a dog here during the beach season.

Niles Veterans' Memorial Waterfall

The Niles Veterans' Memorial Waterfall was built in 1999 as a tribute to residents who died while serving in the military. This waterfall features a large rock formation with multiple water jets at the top.

There is also a large American flag and a separate POW/MIA flag to honor veterans and those who have died or gone missing while in action.

Best Time to Visit: The waterfall hosts a memorial ceremony on Memorial Day and Veterans Day each year.

Pass/Permit/Fees: The waterfall is free to visit.

Closest City or Town: Skokie

How to Get There: From Skokie, head south on Skokie Boulevard and then turn right on Touhy Avenue, crossing the North Branch of the Chicago River into downtown Niles. Take a left onto N Milwaukee Ave, and the falls are on the right at W Touhy Ave &, N Milwaukee Ave.

GPS Coordinates: 42.01189° N, 87.80137° W

Did You Know? Much of Niles's population used to consist of veterans, with the community growing after the Second World War and the Korean War.

Abraham Lincoln Memorial Garden

The Abraham Lincoln Memorial Garden provides a peaceful retreat in the southern end of Springfield. The garden is on 100 acres of woodland on the southeastern shore of Lake Springfield. The garden features about 5 miles of walking paths, with some going along the river. It includes many trees, such as sugar maples and dogwoods. You will also find bur oak and many other fire-resistant trees. There are a few native grasses around the garden, including tallgrass prairie. The big bluestem grass is the most prominent one you can find in the area.

Best Time to Visit: The garden hosts a maple syrup festival in the spring. The festival includes maple syrup produced from some of the trees at the park.

Pass/Permit/Fees: You can visit the garden for free, but donations are encouraged.

Closest City or Town: Springfield

How to Get There: From Springfield, head east on E Myrtle St and turn right onto S 5th St. Continue onto I-55BL S and keep right to stay on I-55BL S. Merge onto I-55 S and take exit 88. Keep left at the fork and follow the signs for E Lake Dr and continue onto E Lake Shore Dr to reach the garden at 2301 E Lake Shore Dr.

GPS Coordinates: 39.69728° N, 89.59680° W

Did You Know? The park includes eight fire pits for evening events. Most of these pits offer views of Lake Springfield.

Abraham Lincoln Presidential Library and Museum

The Abraham Lincoln Presidential Library and Museum in central Springfield honors the iconic United States President and his life, housing exhibits dedicated to Lincoln's boyhood and his ascent to the presidency. You'll also learn about Lincoln's time in the White House, how he led the country during the Civil War and his impact on America since his assassination in 1865. There is also a library housing many documents of Lincoln's work. The museum has replicas of Lincoln's childhood home in Kentucky and parts of the White House exterior. It also features authentic Civil War uniforms and a few of Mary Todd Lincoln's dresses.

Best Time to Visit: The museum is open year-round, but it is especially busy in February near Lincoln's birthday on February 12.

Pass/Permit/Fees: Admission is $15 for adults, $12 for seniors, and $6 for children.

Closest City or Town: Springfield

How to Get There: From Springfield, head west on E Myrtle St, and turn right onto S 4th St. Turn right onto E Lawrence Ave, and then left onto S 6th St to reach 212 N 6th St.

GPS Coordinates: 39.80346° N, 89.64720°W

Did You Know? The theater here hosts various live stage performances, including Civil War ball reenactments.

Air Combat Museum

The Abraham Lincoln Capital Airport in Springfield houses the Air Combat Museum, a site devoted to military aviation. It features many authentic airplanes that were utilized in air combat.

Many of the planes at the museum are in a hangar on the eastern end of the airport, including a Beech AT-11 Kansan, a plane used to train pilots during the Second World War. You'll also find a Beech T-34A Mentor with its detailed cockpit. Some of the planes date back to the 1920s and 1930s. One of the newer planes here is a Soko Galeb G2, the first military plane built in Yugoslavia.

Best Time to Visit: Since the museum is indoors in a hangar, you can visit the museum at any time of the year.

Pass/Permit/Fees: It costs $40 to take a group tour of the museum. Groups can include up to 30 people.

Closest City or Town: Springfield

How to Get There: From Springfield, head south on I-55 S and use exit 100B to merge onto E Sangamon Ave. Keep straight to stay on E Sangamon Ave until you can turn right onto N 5th St. Take a left onto Browning Ave, a right onto J David Jones Pkwy, a left onto Capital Airport Dr, and then another left onto S Airport Dr. After two consecutive rights, you'll reach the museum at 835 S Airport Dr.

GPS Coordinates: 39.84220° N, 89.66568° W

Did You Know? Many of the planes on display here can travel at least 100 miles per hour.

Dana-Thomas House

The Dana-Thomas House in Springfield is one of Frank Lloyd Wright's Prairie School buildings in Illinois. The home was built in 1902 and is open for tours.

The Dana-Thomas House has about 12,000 square feet of space with 35 rooms. The inside features various flat lines and symmetrical patterns to represent the flatlands of the midwestern prairie, a hallmark of Wright's designs. Many of these geometric patterns can be found on the windows.

The house features a Japanese aesthetic and free-standing white oak items all around. These include surfaces where the homeowner's collection of Japanese prints are displayed. The house also has a Torii gate on the inside.

Best Time to Visit: The house is open throughout the year.

Pass/Permit/Fees: The house is free to visit, but a donation is recommended.

Closest City or Town: Springfield

How to Get There: In Springfield, head west on E Myrtle St, turn right, and then left toward S 4th St. Turn right onto S 4th St and turn left onto E Lawrence Ave. Dana Thomas House is on the right at 301 E Lawrence Ave.

GPS Coordinates: 39.79437° N, 89.65151° W

Did You Know? The house features sconces, light fixtures, door panels, and more than 400 windows designed by Wright.

Daughters of Union Veterans of the Civil War Museum

The Daughters of Union Veterans of the Civil War operates a museum in western Springfield, highlighting the history of the war and efforts to preserve many of its historic sites and battlefields. The museum houses various artifacts relating to the Civil War and the Union soldiers who fought. You will find various uniforms, medals, restored photographs, and other historical pieces from that time period and conflict. The Daughters of Union Veterans of the Civil War work to ensure the preservation of Civil War battlefields and monuments to help people learn from the nation's troubled past.

Best Time to Visit: The museum is open throughout the year.

Pass/Permit/Fees: Admission is free, but donations are recommended.

Closest City or Town: Springfield

How to Get There: From Springfield, head west on E Myrtle St and turn right onto S 4th St. Turn left onto E Laurel St, right onto S Lowell Ave, and then left onto S Grand Ave W. Take a final right onto S Walnut St to reach 503 S Walnut St.

GPS Coordinates: 39.79807° N, 89.66374° W

Did You Know? The museum is a few miles from the Old State Capitol building.

Edwards Place Historic Home

The Springfield Art Association operates the Edwards Place Historic Home, an Italianate-style home dating to 1833. This Springfield attraction is decorated with many pieces of Victorian furniture, including a couch from the parlor of the home where Abraham Lincoln and Mary Todd were married. There is also a piano on display that is believed to have been played at Lincoln's wedding.

The house holds a few other Lincoln artifacts, including some related to his funeral. The home hosted guests who came to Springfield for the 1865 event. The M.G. Nelson Family Gallery at the house hosts various art exhibits throughout the year. It also has an art studio with classes for students.

Best Time to Visit: Visit between March and December, as you won't require an appointment to visit the home during those months.

Pass/Permit/Fees: Admission is $5 for children. Children ages ten and under can visit for free.

Closest City or Town: Springfield

How to Get There: In Springfield, head west on E Myrtle St and turn right onto S 4th St to reach the home at 700 N 4th St.

GPS Coordinates: 39.80991° N, 89.65018° W

Did You Know? The home hosts Victorian tea parties with reenactments of Victorian life. These parties are open to groups of at least 25 people.

Elijah Iles House Foundation

The Elijah Iles House Foundation is the oldest house in Springfield. The home was built around 1837 and was home to one of the earliest settlers in the city.

The home features a Greek Revival design, but much of the building reflects a Southern influence. You'll find a timber frame on an extended brick foundation on the outside. The inside features black walnut wood all around.

You'll find furniture from before the Civil War, plus various artifacts relating to Springfield's history. There are also a few watches made by the old Illinois Watch Company on display here.

Best Time to Visit: The house is open year-round.

Pass/Permit/Fees: It is free to visit, but donations are encouraged.

Closest City or Town: Springfield

How to Get There: In Springfield, head west on E Myrtle St and turn right onto S 4th St. Take a right onto E Lawrence Ave, a left onto S 6th St, a right onto E Edwards St, and a right onto S 7th St to reach the house at 628 S 7th St.

GPS Coordinates: 39.79538° N, 89.64642° W

Did You Know? Elijah Iles helped encourage the Sangamon County government to move its seat to Springfield.

Henson Robinson Zoo

You'll find the Henson Robinson Zoo by Lake Springfield, across from the University of Illinois at Springfield campus. The zoo has more than 90 species of animals on display. The zoo contains separate exhibits devoted to animals from different continents, including animals from Africa and Australia. Each habitat features a simulated environment similar to what you'd find in those parts of the world. Some of the animals you will find here include lemurs, cougars, spider monkeys, and African penguins.

Best Time to Visit: The Fur Feather Fin Fall Fling is a popular annual event at the zoo in late September. The event highlights the many ways animals at the zoo prepare for the winter season.

Pass/Permit/Fees: Admission to the zoo is $7 for adults and $5 for children and seniors.

Closest City or Town: Springfield

How to Get There: From Springfield, head east on E Myrtle St and turn right onto S 5th St. Continue onto I-55BL S/I-55BUS S to take a slight left onto Adlai Stevenson Dr. In 2.6 miles, continue onto E Lake Shore Dr, turn right onto Zoo trail and then take a left to reach the zoo at 1100 E Lake Shore Dr.

GPS Coordinates: 39.72761° N, 89.58364° W

Did You Know? The zoo hosts various veterinary doctor practice sessions for students at the nearby University of Illinois at Springfield.

Illinois State Capitol

The Illinois State Capitol is home to the Illinois General Assembly and the office of the Governor of Illinois. You can tour the Capitol and see the many places where the state's government operates. The Capitol features a unique dome designed in the Renaissance Revival style. The building is about 361 feet high, making it the country's tallest capitol that isn't a traditional skyscraper. The capitol grounds include places where the state House of Representatives and Senate operate. These areas are open to visitors during some sessions.

Best Time to Visit: Visit during the Illinois legislative session. The session operates from January to May during most years.

Pass/Permit/Fees: Tours are free, but you may need to reserve a time to visit online.

Closest City or Town: Springfield

How to Get There: In Springfield, head west on E Myrtle St and then turn right onto S 4th St. Take a left onto E Cook St, a right onto S 2nd St, a left onto E Edwards St, and then turn right to reach the capitol parking lot at 840 S Spring St.

GPS Coordinates: 39.79859° N, 89.65542° W

Did You Know? The city of Springfield has a statute stating that no building in the city can be taller than the capitol. One building in Springfield is taller than 361 feet, but it is exempt because it is on lower ground.

Illinois State Museum

The Illinois State Museum is south of the State Capitol Building in downtown Springfield. The museum hosts many exhibits highlighting the history of Illinois.

The museum features a permanent exhibit showcasing stories of people who have lived in the Illinois area for the past 300 years. Visitors learn about how life has changed and how households have evolved. There are also various fossils gathered from around the state at the museum. The museum also includes the Mary Ann MacLean Play Museum, a children's area that includes many interactive exhibits.

Best Time to Visit: The museum offers various temporary exhibitions that change every few months. Check the museum first to see what exhibits are on display before you plan your visit.

Pass/Permit/Fees: Admission to the museum is free.

Closest City or Town: Springfield

How to Get There: In Springfield, head west on E Myrtle St and turn right onto S 4th St. Turn left onto E Cook St, turn right onto S 2nd St, left onto E Edwards St, and then take a right. Take another sharp right to reach the museum parking lot at 502 S Spring St.

GPS Coordinates: 39.79804° N, 89.65571° W

Did You Know? Watch for the Proud Raven Totem Pole standing outside the museum, featuring a wood carving of Abraham Lincoln on the top.

Lincoln Home National Historic Site

The Lincoln Home National Historic Site is a historic house in Springfield that served as the home of Abraham Lincoln from 1844 to 1861. You can tour the house and see many rooms where Lincoln lived. The house has been refurbished to its original state from before Lincoln became president. You'll also find many other nearby houses that were important to Lincoln. The area includes part of the Underground Railroad and a house that was once home to prominent philanthropist Julius Rosenwald.

Best Time to Visit: The home is open throughout the year, but it is very popular in February around Lincoln's birthday.

Pass/Permit/Fees: The house is free to visit. Robert Todd Lincoln donated the home to the state in 1887 under the rule that it would be open to the public for free.

Closest City or Town: Springfield

How to Get There: In Springfield, head west on E Myrtle St and turn right onto S 4th St. Take a right onto E Lawrence Ave, a left onto S 6th St, a right onto E Capitol Ave, a right onto S 7th St, and then turn left to reach the Lincoln Home Parking lot at S 8th St. From the parking lot, head north and turn right onto E Jackson St, take a left onto S 8th St to reach the home. It's about a two minute walk.

GPS Coordinates: 39.79755° N, 89.64494° W

Did You Know? Many of the houses at the site were for members of the Whig Party, the political party that Lincoln belonged to before the formation of the Republican Party.

Lincoln's New Salem

Menard County in northwestern Springfield houses Lincoln's New Salem, a reconstruction of the former Kentucky village where Abraham Lincoln grew up. You can walk the grounds of New Salem to learn about where Lincoln lived and some of his experiences before becoming president. This includes a replica of a store where he worked as a clerk and a workshop where he split rails.

The New Salem site features 12 log houses, ten workshops, a tavern, and a school that holds church services. The buildings illustrate life in the 1830s when Lincoln was elected to the Illinois General Assembly.

Best Time to Visit: This attraction is open all year, but try to visit between May and October if possible.

Pass/Permit/Fees: It is free to visit New Salem, but donations are encouraged.

Closest City or Town: Springfield

How to Get There: From downtown Springfield, go northwest on Highway 97, continuing right in Farmingdale. Keep following the highway north through Salisbury. Turn right on Lincoln's New Salem Road to reach 15558 History Ln.

GPS Coordinates: 39.97904° N, 89.84720° W

Did You Know? The settlement features a small-scale model of the Talisman steamboat. Lincoln worked on this boat for a brief period in the early 1830s.

Lincoln Tomb

The Oak Ridge Cemetery in Springfield is home to the final resting place of President Abraham Lincoln. Lincoln's tomb is in the central part of the cemetery.

Lincoln's tomb features a 117-foot obelisk and various statues around the base. The front features a recasting of Gutzon Borglum's bust of Lincoln's head at the United States Capitol. Lincoln is buried in a room in the tomb with a red marble cenotaph in the middle. The tomb is also the final resting place of Mary Todd Lincoln and three of their sons.

Best Time to Visit: The tomb is popular around February, the month of Lincoln's birth.

Pass/Permit/Fees: You can visit the tomb for free.

Closest City or Town: Springfield

How to Get There: In Springfield, head west on E Myrtle St and turn right onto S 4th St. Turn left onto E Cook St, turn right onto S 2nd St, turn left onto N Grand Ave E, and then turn right onto Monument Ave. Continue straight and then take a left at the "Y." Take a sharp right to enter the parking lot at 1500 Monument Avenue Cemetery.

GPS Coordinates: 39.82285° N, 89.65667° W

Did You Know? Lincoln's tomb opened in 1874, 9 years after his death. His remains have been moved over the years to prevent criminals from trying to steal his body. Lincoln's first resting place is also marked north of the tomb.

Margery Adams Wildlife Sanctuary

The Margery Adams Wildlife Sanctuary is a refuge in Springfield run by the Audubon Society. The sanctuary is centered around a nineteenth-century home. The 40-acre sanctuary features four separate walking trails, including many that connect to bird habitats. At least 80 species of birds have been found at the sanctuary. You'll also find coyotes, opossums, raccoons, and many other forms of wildlife in the wood area.

The Prairie Restoration Project to the north features various open grass spaces. This section is part of an extensive project to restore the trees, grasses, and other features in the area to return to their nineteenth-century forms.

Best Time to Visit: Visit during the summer, as you may find various migratory birds.

Pass/Permit/Fees: It is free to visit the sanctuary.

Closest City or Town: Springfield

How to Get There: From Springfield, head south on I-55 S/I-72 W, and then take exit 96B for IL-29 N toward S Grand Ave. Merge onto IL-29 W, turn right onto S Dirksen Pkwy, and then turn left onto IL-97 N/E Clear Lake Ave to reach the sanctuary on the right at 2315 E Clear Lake Ave.

GPS Coordinates: 39.80239° N, 89.61990° W

Did You Know? The reserve features a few areas with tallgrass prairie. There were once more than 20 million acres of prairie grass throughout Illinois, but only a few thousand acres remain today.

Old State Capitol

The Old State Capitol is a Greek Revival dome building in downtown Springfield. The building was Illinois's state house from 1840 to 1876. The Old State Capitol is where Abraham Lincoln appeared as a lawyer before the state Supreme Court. He made his House Divided speech here in 1858, and his body was presented in state here after his death in 1865. Barack Obama also announced his presidential candidacy here in 2007.

The capitol features the old House of Representatives floor and the governor's old office. Tours include the state Supreme Court room where Lincoln pled many cases.

Best Time to Visit: The venue is open throughout the year, but it may be closed at times when the building is undergoing restoration.

Pass/Permit/Fees: You can visit the building for free, but reservations are required.

Closest City or Town: Springfield

How to Get There: In Springfield, head west on E Myrtle St and turn right onto S 4th St. Take a right onto E Washington Ave to reach the Old State Capitol at 1 N Old State Capitol Plaza.

GPS Coordinates: 39.80113° N, 89.64859° W

Did You Know? Springfield was named the capital of Illinois in 1838 because it is in the geographic center of the state.

Springfield and Central Illinois African-American History Museum

The Springfield and Central Illinois African-American History Museum is near the southeastern end of the Oak Ridge Cemetery. The museum features many exhibits dedicated to the Black experience and history in Illinois. The museum includes stories of the Springfield Race Riot of 1908 and African-American churches and pioneers who settled Illinois when it first became a state.

The museum also hosts an exhibit about President Barack Obama, featuring artifacts related to his presidency, including various texts and letters.

Best Time to Visit: The museum is open year-round, but the specific exhibits on display will change throughout the year. Check with the museum first to see what is open.

Pass/Permit/Fees: Admission is free, but donations are encouraged.

Closest City or Town: Springfield

How to Get There: In Springfield, take N 9th Street from downtown Springfield and turn left on N Grand Ave E. Turn right onto Monument Ave and continue straight until you reach the museum on the right at 1440 Monument Ave.

GPS Coordinates: 39.82018° N, 89.65368° W

Did You Know? The History Comes Alive series at the museum offers conversations and meetings with many history scholars and experts.

Vachel Lindsay Home

This Springfield attraction was the longtime home of Vachel Lindsay, a pioneer of singing poetry. Built in 1848, the home hosts a museum dedicated to Lindsay's life and work. Visitors can see the bed where he was born and the desk where he wrote many of his poems.

Much of the house reflects Lindsay's poetry and how he used colloquial language in his poems to create a style that turned poetry into a performance art.

Best Time to Visit: The house is open during the afternoon hours in the spring and summer.

Pass/Permit/Fees: Tickets are $10 per person.

Closest City or Town: Springfield

How to Get There: In Springfield, take W Cook Street and head south on S MacArthur Blvd. Turn left onto W Lawrence Ave, left onto S 4th St, and right onto E Edwards St to reach the home on the left at 603 S 5th St.

GPS Coordinates: 39.79613° N, 89.64970° W

Did You Know? Lindsay lived in this home for his entire life, from his birth in 1879 to his death in 1931.

Washington Park Botanical Garden

You'll find the Washington Park Botanical Garden in Springfield's western end. The garden features more than 1,200 plant species on display.

The park also includes an indoor greenhouse with separate sections devoted to South American rainforests and tropical jungles from Africa and Asia. One of the most popular gardens features more than 5,000 roses.

The Angel of Hope statue is one of the most prominent features of the garden. The statue is dedicated to children who have passed away with a surrounding memorial wall that is updated annually with the names of local children who have died.

Best Time to Visit: The garden offers various seasonal displays. The Easter lily display in the spring is the most popular.

Pass/Permit/Fees: Admission to the garden is free.

Closest City or Town: Springfield

How to Get There: In Springfield, from I-55BUS, head south onto S 5th St and turn right onto E Laurel St. Turn right onto S MacArther Blvd, left onto W Fayette Ave, and then take two consecutive lefts to reach the park at 1740 W Fayette Ave.

GPS Coordinates: 39.78943° N, 89.68464° W

Did You Know? The garden has a massive carillon with cast bronze bells at the top.

Anderson Japanese Gardens

The Anderson Japanese Gardens in Rockford is a 12-acre area that features various waterfalls, ponds, and rock formations. It uses water to represent life-giving forces, while the plants represent the world's natural energy.

You will find Japanese maple plants and cloud pines throughout the gardens. You'll also find many fish in the water, with some areas featuring beetle traps near the surface to encourage the fish to leave the water for food.

Best Time to Visit: Visit early in the day for the most serene experience. The gardens open at eight in the morning.

Pass/Permit/Fees: It costs $11 for an adult to enter. Seniors cost $10, and children cost $9.

Closest City or Town: Rockford

How to Get There: Go north on IL-251 from downtown Rockford, then go right on Spring Creek Road. You can also reach IL-251 from I-90 by taking the exit to US-20 and going west into Rockford, turning right on 3rd Street, and then merging on 2nd Street to IL-251.

GPS Coordinates: 42.29025° N, 89.05781° W

Did You Know? The garden features a small café that offers farm-to-table foods.

Burpee Museum of Natural History

You will find the Burpee Museum of Natural History on the northern end of the Rock River near the Whitman Street Bridge in Rockford. The venue is spread across four buildings, one of them being an 1852 mansion.

The most popular exhibit at the Burpee Museum is Jane, a juvenile Tyrannosaurus rex skeleton. The skeleton is about 21 feet long and includes 17 teeth. You'll also find a scale cast of a 40-foot adult Tyrannosaurus rex near Jane. Other exhibits at the museum include a look at prehistoric life in the Rockford area and how various rock formations were created. A re-creation of a prehistoric coal forest is also on display here.

Best Time to Visit: The museum houses various seasonal exhibits, so check the museum to see what is appearing here before you make your visit.

Pass/Permit/Fees: Adults cost $10 to enter, while children cost $8.

Closest City or Town: Rockford

How to Get There: In Rockford, head northwest on W State St and turn right onto N Main St. Turn right at Fisher Ave and then take another right to reach the museum at 737 N Main St.

GPS Coordinates: 42.27750° N, 89.08814° W

Did You Know? Although the Jane skeleton has a female name, the exact gender of the Tyrannosaurus rex skeleton is unknown.

Castle Rock State Park

Castle Rock State Park is near the town of Oregon, south of Rockford on the Rock River. The park has various overlooks of the Rock River, including a few close to 100 feet in height, and features many massive sandstone formations.

There are also eight walking trails around the park that are popular for cross-country skiing and tobogganing during the winter. There are also a few nature preserves surrounding the outside parts of the park, along with a boating ramp near the northern end of the river.

Best Time to Visit: The park is open throughout the year.

Pass/Permit/Fees: You can visit for free, but contact the park first if you wish to bring your boat to the dock. Larger boats may not fit in the river, as the water varies in depth.

Closest City or Town: Rockford

How to Get There: From Rockford, follow S Main St and turn onto S Springfield Ave. Take a left onto Prairie Rd and then turn right onto IL-2 S. miles. In 22.9 miles, the park is on the right at 1365 W Castle Rd.

GPS Coordinates: 41.97789° N, 89.36377° W

Did You Know? Many of the trees across the river from the park are a part of the Lowden-Miller State Forest.

Discovery Center Museum

The Discovery Center Museum is in the Riverfront Museum Park region of downtown Rockford. The museum houses exhibits and workshops for children, many of them dedicated to agriculture, science, and technology. There's an exhibit on how farm equipment works and a site highlighting how color and light are produced. Another section features a look at the science of sports and an interactive exhibit on how bubbles are formed.

The Rock River Discovery Park is outside the museum and showcases an 8-foot water wheel. Kids will find many slides, swings, and other interactive features throughout the park. The area also hosts various arts and crafts workshops during the year.

Best Time to Visit: The museum hosts art workshops, science experiments, and other fun features for children. Check the museum to see what is planned.

Pass/Permit/Fees: One adult and one child can enter the museum for $20.

Closest City or Town: Rockford

How to Get There: In Rockford, head northwest on W State St and turn right onto N Main St to reach the museum at 711 N Main St.

GPS Coordinates: 42.27721° N, 89.08939° W

Did You Know? The museum has an exhibit dedicated to Janice Voss, an astronaut, and Rockford native. Voss was in space for 49 days.

Hurricane Harbor Rockford

The Six Flags amusement park company runs a water park in the Rockford suburb of Cherry Valley called Six Flags Hurricane Harbor Rockford. The park was originally called Magic Waters. The water park includes 12 water slides and three pools. The Typhoon Terror ride is 230 feet long and features a giant funnel. The Tropical Twisters slides drop down five stories. You can also enjoy the Abyss, a dark slide ride. The park holds various concerts and other family-friendly events throughout the season. There are also a few dining spots around the park.

Best Time to Visit: The park is open from May through Labor Day.

Pass/Permit/Fees: Daily ticket prices will vary, but tickets are $20 in most cases.

Closest City or Town: Rockford

How to Get There: From Rockford, head east on I-39 N and take exit 122B to merge onto US-20 W. Use the middle lane to continue on Harrison Ave. Turn right onto S Mall Dr, take a slight right and turn right onto S Bell School Rd. Turn right onto Mid Mall Dr, right at Cherryvale N Blvd, and then left to reach 7820 Cherryvale N Blvd.

GPS Coordinates: 42.24634° N, 88.96275° W

Did You Know? Six Flags also operates the Great America amusement park in the northern Chicago suburb of Gurnee. Great America also has a Hurricane Harbor water park location.

Klehm Arboretum and Botanic Garden

The Klehm Arboretum and Botanic Garden in Rockford is on more than 150 acres of land and features more than 50 species of trees. These include many trees that represent Europe and Africa.

Some of the trees at the arboretum are bur oak trees, including ones that were planted here prior to people settling in the Rockford area. Some of the trees are at least 300 years old. The garden section of the arboretum features a butterfly garden, children's garden, and prehistoric garden. The prehistoric section contains mosses, ferns, ginkgo, and many other plants that grew in the area millions of years ago.

Best Time to Visit: The arboretum is popular in the fall, as the orange and yellow colors of the trees will be on full display then.

Pass/Permit/Fees: Adult admission is $8, while admission for children and seniors is $5.

Closest City or Town: Rockford

How to Get There: From Rockford, head northwest on W State St and turn left onto S Main St. Take a right onto Clifton Ave, and then take two consecutive lefts to reach the garden at 2715 S Main St.

GPS Coordinates: 42.24465° N, 89.11255° W

Did You Know? The arboretum has an extensive array of cork trees from East Asia.

Lake Le-Aqua-Na State Park

Lake Le-Aqua-Na State Park in the northwestern Illinois town of Lena features a 40-acre lake and wooded spaces with several walking trails, including one that goes around the entire lake.

The area is popular among birding enthusiasts. You can find various birds throughout the park, including some eagles and hawks. The park also has a swimming area and a nearby fishing pier. There are a few camping sites in the area, including an equestrian camping site.

Best Time to Visit: Visit during the spring or summer, as it is easier for you to find more birds in the area during this time.

Pass/Permit/Fees: The park is free to visit, but it may cost money to rent some equipment.

Closest City or Town: Rockford

How to Get There: From Rockford, head east on US-20 E and turn left onto IL-73 N. Take a left onto W Lena St, a right onto N Freedom St, and then continue onto N Lake Rd. Take two consecutive lefts and a right to reach the parking lot near the lake.

GPS Coordinates: 42.41993° N, 89.82693° W

Did You Know? The largemouth bass and bullhead populations inside the lake are self-sustaining. The park operators still add walleye and a few other fish on occasion, but many of the fish here are native to the park.

Midway Village and Museum Center

You'll see many intriguing historical artifacts and reenactments at the Midway Village and Museum Center in Rockford. The center highlights life in early twentieth-century Rockford, including how the city served in the First World War.

You will also learn about transportation in the area and how the city of Rockford evolved over the years. The center also has various events.

Best Time to Visit: The center hosts an art show at the start of each month. You'll see live artists composing their latest pieces at the center.

Pass/Permit/Fees: Admission is $8 for adults and $6 for children.

Closest City or Town: Rockford

How to Get There: In Rockford, head northwest on W State St and turn right onto N Main St. Take a slight right onto Harlem Blvd, right onto Auburn St, and then continue onto Spring Creek Rd. Turn right onto N Mulford Rd, left onto Guilford Rd, and then turn right to reach the museum at 6799 Guilford Rd.

GPS Coordinates: 42.28065° N, 88.98434° W

Did You Know? The museum also houses a memorial dedicated to local soldiers who died in the Vietnam War. The memorial is a scale model of the Vietnam Memorial in Washington, D.C.

Nicholas Conservatory and Gardens

The Nicholas Conservatory and Gardens is on the southern end of the Rock River in Rockford. The garden features 11,000 square feet of indoor garden space.

The venue focuses on tropical plants, unique trees, bushes, and other flora in an indoor lagoon environment. The glass atrium provides the natural light these plants require, while the humid climate ensures their survival.

The venue offers various exhibits dedicated to many unique aspects of nature. Some of these exhibits include a butterfly garden as well as a section highlighting carnivorous plants.

Best Time to Visit: Tuesdays are a great time to visit, as the conservatory hosts a food truck rodeo on that day.

Pass/Permit/Fees: Tickets are $9 for adults and $7 for seniors, children, and veterans. Tickets are $2 cheaper for Rockford residents.

Closest City or Town: Rockford

How to Get There: In Rockford, head southeast on W State St and turn left onto IL-251 N/N 3rd St. Turn left onto Ethel Ave, and then take a right in 197 ft to reach the conservatory at 1354 N 2nd St.

GPS Coordinates: 42.28258° N, 89.07072° W

Did You Know?
The garden operates a model train throughout the conservatory every December and January, paying tribute to Rockford's history in the rail industry.

Prairie Street Brewhouse

The Prairie Street Brewhouse in Rockford is one of Illinois's top culinary attractions. The brewhouse is on the Rock River and has been producing beer on site since 2013.

The brewhouse offers various beers for sale, including the Wavey Blonde, Peacock Pale Ale, and the Prairie Street IPA. The beers are produced in a warehouse founded in the mid-nineteenth century. The brewery also offers various seasonal beers and special releases.

Best Time to Visit: Visit during the evening, as the brewhouse often has live music events then.

Pass/Permit/Fees: The dining area is free to visit, but it costs money to purchase beer or food. Reservations may be required for some occasions.

Closest City or Town: Rockford

How to Get There: The brewhouse is two blocks north of Jefferson Street in downtown Rockford. It is on the southern shore of the Rock River. Out-of-town visitors can take I-90 to Rockford and exit onto US-20, eventually going north on Main Street to reach downtown.

GPS Coordinates: 42.27344° N, 89.08749° W

Did You Know? The dockside part of the brewhouse contains a vast pinball arcade featuring many games from the past and present.

Rock Cut State Park

Rock Cut State Park is a 3,000-acre park northeast of Rockford in Winnebago County. The park features more than 250 campsites that are open during all seasons.

The park offers about 40 miles of trails, mostly for mountain biking, but there are also 14 miles of trails for horseback riding.

Pierce Lake is in the middle of the park. The lake is open for fishing, as it is regularly restocked. There are more than a hundred varieties of flowers found around the park, as well as wildlife, including deer, woodchucks, raccoons, and squirrels.

Best Time to Visit: The fall and spring are the best times to visit, as conditions can get too extreme during the summer and winter seasons.

Pass/Permit/Fees: The park is free to visit, although it may cost extra to rent a bike or campsite. The park does not offer horses for rent.

Closest City or Town: Rockford

How to Get There: In Rockford, head down I-90 W and take the IL-173/I-90 W exit. Take a left in 0.7 miles, a left onto Hart Rd, an immediate right and then another right to reach 7318 Harlem Rd.

GPS Coordinates: 42.35406° N, 88.98610° W

Did You Know? The hardwood trees around the park offer beautiful colors in the fall.

Rockford City Market

The Rockford City Market features products from many local businesses. The market hosts various local eateries, farm goods vendors, and fashion and accessory retailers.

The Market Building includes numerous rotating vendors throughout the year that specialize in different seasonal activities.

There is also a creative studio at the City Market. Artists can rent the studio and use it for many art projects, including photography.

Best Time to Visit: The market is open from Tuesday to Sunday. The market hosts produce farmers every Saturday morning.

Pass/Permit/Fees: It is free to visit the market, but each vendor will charge its own rates for products.

Closest City or Town: Rockford

How to Get There: Take US-20 in either direction to downtown Rockford. The market is on Madison Street in between Market and State streets. The 1st Street and East State station on the RMTD 11, 12, and 14 bus routes is the nearest transit station to the market.

GPS Coordinates: 42.26951° N, 89.08972° W

Did You Know? The market's Incubator Kitchen offers many pieces of commercial-grade cooking equipment that people can use when starting new restaurants, catering businesses, or food trucks.

Tinker Swiss Cottage

The Tinker Swiss Cottage is near Kent Creek in southern Rockford. The cottage is a Swiss-style house built in 1865, featuring 27 rooms and a beautiful outdoor garden.

You'll notice various angled roofs with high ceilings, distinct multi-tone wood panels, and even a spiral staircase made from one piece of wood. The inside also houses various nineteenth-century pieces of furniture and art and other objects from the Tinker family.

Best Time to Visit: The cottage offers monthly Haunted Rockford events, usually during the second or third week of the month. These events highlight paranormal studies and include conversations and tours.

Pass/Permit/Fees: Admission is $8 for adults and $5 for children. Ticket prices for other occasions will vary by event.

Closest City or Town: Rockford

How to Get There: The house is south of downtown Rockford. Go south on Main Street from the city center and take a right on Morgan Street, then right on Winnebago Street, and then right on Blake Street. Blake St turns into S Court St, and 411 Kent St is on the left.

GPS Coordinates: 42.26444° N, 89.10282° W

Did You Know? The cottage is named for Robert Hall Tinker, a resident who built the home after being inspired during his travels in Europe.

Zip Rockford

Zip-lining is a popular recreational activity that you can enjoy at Zip Rockford. Located near the Rockford University campus, the venue features five zip lines ranging from 150 to 1,000 feet long. The two longest lines are dual racing lines that feature separate lanes.

This attraction also features a 75-foot suspension bridge. The bridge wobbles and shakes with narrow planks, requiring the best balance and coordination to make it across. There is also an outdoor education yurt on the southern end of the complex. The site highlights the many beautiful natural features in the Rockford area.

Best Time to Visit: Zip Rockford is open from Wednesday to Sunday. The Zombie Zip Tour is open in October and features a haunted theme.

Pass/Permit/Fees: Each tour costs $39 per person. Zip Rockford strongly encourages reservations.

Closest City or Town: Rockford

How to Get There: In Rockford, head down 1st Ave toward S Longwood St. Turn right onto E State St. Turn right onto S Alpine Rd, right onto Larson Ave, and then another right onto Shenandoah Ave to reach 4402 Larson Ave on the right.

GPS Coordinates: 42.25922° N, 89.03115° W

Did You Know? Zip Rockford features lines built by EBL Zipline Tours, a group with various zip-lining sites around the United States and Canada.

Illinois Beach State Park

The Illinois Beach State Park is located in the northeastern end of the state near Zion. The park features more than 4,000 acres of land for various activities and covers 6 miles of shoreline on Lake Michigan. You'll find many dunes and swales throughout the park. Plus, you'll see nearly 600 hundred varieties of plants in the area.

Most of the nature trails at the park are in the south near the Dead River. The northern area features a nature preserve and a marina. The North Point Marina holds room for fishing boats and other vessels at the northern end near the Wisconsin state border.

Best Time to Visit: The spring is a relatively quiet time to visit the area.

Pass/Permit/Fees: It is free to enter the park, although you might need to get a reservation for some activities.

Closest City or Town: Zion

How to Get There: In Zion, head east on 27th St and turn right onto IL-137 S/Sheridan Rd. Turn left onto W Wadsworth Rd, continue straight onto Illinois Beach State Park and then onto Patomos Ave. Turn right onto Lake Front Dr to reach the park on the right.

GPS Coordinates: 42.42385° N, 87.80531° W

Did You Know? The Dead River is very short, as it is blocked by sandbars produced by waves from around Lake Michigan.

Proper Planning

With this guide, you are well on your way to properly planning a marvelous adventure. When you plan your travels, you should become familiar with the area, save any maps to your phone for access without internet, and bring plenty of water—especially during the summer months. Depending on the adventure you choose, you will also want to bring snacks and even a lunch. For younger children, you should do your research and find destinations that best suits your family's needs. Additionally, you should also plan when to get gas, local lodgings, and where to get food after you're finished. We've done our best to group these destinations based on nearby towns and cities to help make planning easier.

Dangerous Wildlife

There are several dangerous animals and insects you may encounter while hiking. With a good dose of caution and awareness, you can explore safely. Here is what you can do to keep yourself and your loved ones safe from dangerous flora and fauna while exploring:

- Keep to the established trails.
- Do not look under rocks, leaves, or sticks.
- Keep hands and feet out of small crawl spaces, bushes, covered areas, or crevices.
- Wear long sleeves and pants to keep arms and legs protected.
- Keep your distance should you encounter any dangerous wildlife or plants.

Limited Cell Service

Do not rely on cell service for navigation or emergencies. Always have a map with you and let someone know where you are and for how long you intend to be gone, just in case.

First Aid Information

Always travel with a first aid kit with you in case of emergencies.

Here are items to be certain to include in your primary first aid kit:

- Nitrile gloves
- Blister care products
- Band-aids - multiple sizes and waterproof type
- Ace wrap and athletic tape
- Alcohol wipes and antibiotic ointment
- Irrigation syringe
- Tweezers, nail clippers, trauma shears, safety pins
- Small Ziplock bags containing contaminated trash

It is recommended to also keep a secondary first aid kit, especially when hiking, for more serious injuries or medical emergencies. Items in this should include:

- Blood clotting sponges
- Sterile gauze pads
- Trauma pads
- Second-skin/burn treatment
- Triangular bandages/sling
- Butterfly strips
- Tincture of benzoin

- Medications (ibuprofen, acetaminophen, antihistamine, aspirin, etc.)
- Thermometer
- CPR mask
- Wilderness medicine handbook
- Antivenin

There is so much more to explore, but this is a great start.

For information on all national parks, visit: www.nps.gov.

This site will give you information on up-to-date entrance fees and how to purchase a park pass for unlimited access to national and state parks. This site will also introduce you to all of the trails of each park.

Always check before you travel to destinations to make sure there are no closures. Some hikes close when there is heavy rain or snow in the area, and other parks close parts of their land for the migration of wildlife. Attractions may change their hours or temporarily shut down for various reasons. Check the websites for the most up-to-date information.

Made in the USA
Monee, IL
26 November 2024

71311474R00077